LAUGHING

at

WALL STREET

LAUGHING
at
WALL STREET

How I Beat the Pros at Investing
(by Reading Tabloids, Shopping at the Mall,
and Connecting on Facebook)
and How You Can, Too

CHRIS CAMILLO

St. Martin's Press New York

Library of Congress Cataloging-in-Publication Data

Camillo, Chris.

   Laughing at Wall Street : how I beat the pros at investing (by reading tabloids, shopping at the mall, and connecting on facebook) and how you can too / Chris Camillo. — 1st ed.

         p. cm.

   Includes bibliographical references and index.

   ISBN 978-0-312-65785-7 (hardback)

   1. Stocks.   2. Investments.   3. Investment analysis.   I. Title.

   HG4661.C322 2011

   332.63'22—dc23   2011025856

First Edition: November 2011

10   9   8   7   6   5   4   3   2   1

To Emerson and Owen—

While you were only recently brought into this world, I share the stories in this book with the hope that you will someday embrace their lessons to realize your own investment successes, and that your success provides you with the financial independence and means to enact positive changes on your world.

Learn to take big risks. Learn to survive big failures. But most importantly, learn how to win big in life—so you can give back even bigger.

To learn about Chris Camillo's ongoing commitment to charitable giving, visit ChrisCamillo.com.

Contents

CONTENTS

Preface

People may doubt what you say,
but they will believe what you do.
—LEWIS CASS

From September 2007 to the completion of this book in April 2010, the value of my self-managed investment portfolio appreciated from $83,752 to $2,388,311. A schedule of my investment returns for this period of time, as confirmed by the independent accounting firm Wagner, Eubank & Nichols, LLP, are available for public viewing on ChrisCamillo.com.

Introduction

Does the idea of investing in the stock market intimidate you?

Do you change the channel every time a financial talking head appears on the TV screen and regurgitates some meaningless Wall Street jargon?

Do business cable networks put you to sleep?

If you are at all like me, your answers to these three questions are yes, yes, and yes!

But here's a much more important question for you: Do you feel that you don't have enough time, money, knowledge, or skill to start investing—so you don't?

If your answer to that question is also yes, I am here to change that answer.

I am not a stockbroker. Nor am I a financial analyst, a Wall Street trader, or a hedge fund manager. In fact, aside from two briefly held college internships, I have never even worked in the financial industry.

I don't hold an MBA, I have never attended an Ivy League school, and, despite many offers, I certainly have never received money for financial advice.

What I am is a self-directed or "amateur" investor. Yet I don't crunch numbers, I don't study charts, and I don't analyze the balance sheets of the companies whose stocks I buy. I rarely even read the *Wall Street Journal*.

I bought and sold my first stock at the age of twelve, by picking a ticker symbol at random from the Business section of my dad's morning newspaper. That was more than twenty years ago. Today, using a more refined and sensible—but nearly as simple—stock-picking methodology, I manage for myself one of the world's top-ranked personal investment portfolios.

Over the past three years the value of my self-managed personal stock portfolio has grown twentyfold from less than $100,000 to over $2 million. This includes a period from 2008 to 2009 commonly referred to as the Great Financial Collapse, when the value of the stock market, along with most all publicly traded stocks, was cut in half.

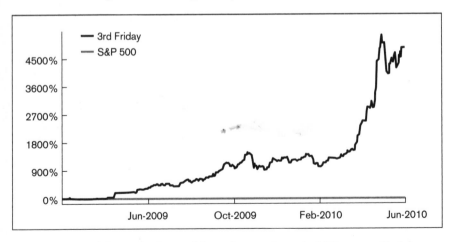

Snapshot of the author's portfolio taken on June 2, 2010, as verified by Covestor.com.

The steep ascending line in this graph represents the twelve-month performance of my personal stock portfolio from June 2009 through June 2010. (The label "3rd Friday" refers to my Internet alias; you'll learn about its meaning later.) The flat line at the bottom of the graph represents the performance of the S&P 500 stocks—basically the performance of the stock market as a whole—which nearly mirrors the performance of most "professionally" managed portfolios.

If the difference between the two lines seems extreme, that's because it is. In 2010, of the forty thousand-plus portfolios tracked globally by Covester.com (the world's largest portfolio tracking service), my portfolio was ranked number one among all those with a value exceeding $250,000.

So, if an ordinary guy like me, who despises traditional, mind-numbing financial analysis, is able to outdo the Wall Street "experts," my question is, why can't you?

You say you don't like math? No problem! Short on time? Who isn't? Whether you are a schoolteacher, a physician, a retail clerk, or a creative type with zero financial literacy, I will show you how you can help your family and improve your long-term financial future by becoming a successful self-directed investor.

Documented studies have proven again and again that there is no correlation between one's ability to pick winning stocks and one's level of financial knowledge or experience. In more than a hundred contests held by *The Wall Street Journal* since 1988, professional money managers have not been able to outperform either the stock market at large or stocks chosen by darts thrown by *Journal* staff members at a newspaper's financial pages.

Fortunately, my recipe for success centers on you, and not on your scholarly degree or level of financial expertise.

Do you watch TV, read magazines, connect with friends on Facebook, or surf the Web? Do you frequent the mall, eat out, or shop for groceries? Do you have children in your family or extended family? Do you spend your daytime hours anywhere other than a Wall Street trading room?

If you answered yes to any of these questions, you have what it takes to become a successful self-directed investor. You might very well be an outsider to Wall Street and "all things financial," but unlike the Wall Street suits who spend their days staring at flashing ticker symbols on computer screens, you have your feet deeply planted in the real world. Because of that, you have firsthand exposure to the companies, products, and trends that shape winning investments in both good times and bad.

Have you ever waited forty minutes to get seated at a newly opened P.F. Chang's or a Cheesecake Factory restaurant in the suburbs? It can be a frustrating experience, I know. That is, unless you own stock in either of these companies—in which case you would welcome the long wait times and have ample profits to afford their $8 cocktails.

Do you have a teenage daughter who has begged you for a pair of overpriced (at least so I think) Ugg boots or True Religion jeans because "everyone's getting them"? How about a teenage son who spends all hours of the day and night playing Guitar Hero?

If you don't have those very typical teenagers living in your home, I'm willing to bet that you have a family member, friend, or colleague at work who does—meaning that you have had an opportunity to spot these emerging youth trends long before they became evident to the overworked investment analysts on Wall Street who are preoccupied with examining every number that corporations can throw at them.

If you watch nightly entertainment news programs or read weekly tabloids, you might recall seeing or reading about Michelle Obama mentioning on *The Tonight Show* that she and her children love to shop at J.Crew. Her public endorsement of the brand caused sales to spike. The retailer's stock price soon followed.

Did you happen to visit an amusement park or state fair during the summer of 2006? If so, I'll bet you noticed more than a family or two sporting brightly colored rubber Crocs sandals. You may have been wearing a pair yourself at the time. As bright as those rubber sandals were, the sharply dressed tycoons on Wall Street never saw them coming—until they read about the company's record sales in the Business pages.

These examples all show that anyone, regardless of his professional or educational background, can leverage both surroundings and relationships to become a great stock picker. Hedge fund analysts spend exorbitant amounts of money polling "real people" and researching industry "experts" to gather outdated insight into the information you already have at your fingertips. I know this because for the past decade my day job has been working at e-Rewards Market Research to build and manage what has become the world's largest market research panel. Those analysts who are trying to get inside your head were my company's clients.

This book will teach you how to view your world through "investor's glasses." I will not use financial or technical jargon you don't understand, or ask you to break out your financial calculator, either.

What I will do is improve your financial well-being by showing you how to take advantage of the innate observational and investigative skills you already have. You will learn from the experiences and real-world stories of successful amateur investors from varied professional backgrounds and age groups.

Investing might not be my profession, but it is my passion. It has the power to bring excitement and purpose even to the most mundane aspects of my daily life. What has made it a passion for me is that it does not interfere with but in fact enriches my personal, family, and professional relationships. Best of all, it has for years earned me more money on an annual basis than my day job.

Whether you are dabbling with a few hundred dollars or intent on making millions, there has never been a more exciting time to become a self-directed investor. My own mother recently opened an online brokerage account and paid just $7 in commission to make her first stock purchase at the age of sixty-three. A female colleague of mine, who is also a "super-mom," doubled the value of her investment portfolio this year on her very first stock pick. Her children, ages four and eight, have become her secret weapons as members of her trend-spotting team.

In the coming chapters I will show you the stock-picking advantages you have over financial professionals and how to generate life-changing profits from those advantages in a way that is fun and easy—all in your spare time, beginning with as little or as much money as you choose. And if you don't have money to invest, do not fear. I will even show you how to find investment money you didn't know you had.

1

"EENY, MEENY, MINEY, MO"

Investments of a Twelve-year-old

"Dad, Dad, Dad! I'm going to be rich!" I screamed as I burst un-invited into my parents' bathroom waving a copy of *The Wall Street Journal* in the air.

I was twelve years old and, like a lot of other boys growing up on Long Island, usually spent most of what little money I had on base-ball cards. That was until that morning, when I came to the realiza-tion that, for years, I had been throwing my allowance away on a mass-produced pseudo-investment that would likely never substan-tially increase in value. Much of my adolescence had been spent ana-lyzing baseball player stats and negotiating card trades with friends and fellow collectors at swap meets—and for what? Even my prized 1984 baseball card set had barely appreciated in value for two years! I had mistaken a hobby for investing. When I realized this, I swore that the industry would never get another dime of my hard-earned money. I decided it was time I graduated to the big leagues of investing.

Hopping atop my parents' bathroom vanity that early December morning, I ripped open *The Wall Street Journal* to enlighten my father on my groundbreaking discovery.

Amid pages of micro-type stock quotes I had encircled the stock symbol for Toys"R"Us.

"Twenty-two days till Christmas!" I announced. "Just think of all the Christmas and Hanukkah toys parents will be buying in the next few weeks! I'm telling you, Dad, this is a sure thing!"

I then handed my father a fist-size roll of $1 and $5 bills—representing months of hoarding my allowance and birthday cash—and urged him to help me facilitate the purchase of stock in Toys"R"Us. "Quick, Dad! Call your broker!"

My father, a lawyer, had limited investing experience, but he was wise enough not to take my money. Instead, he taught me an important lesson in stock investing I would never forget. He explained that the price of Toys"R"Us stock already reflected all widely known information about the company including past, present, and anticipated future sales. I learned that the price of the company's stock, much like the stock price of other companies that benefit from holiday sales, does not go up in value each holiday season—as investors already anticipate that the company will sell more toys at that time of year. A decade later I would relearn this lesson while studying the "efficient markets theory" in business school. The theory asserts that it is not possible for a person to achieve investment returns greater than average market returns, given the information publicly available at the time of the investment.

"But then how do you know," I asked my father, "when to buy a company's stock?"

"That depends," he replied. "The very best time to buy a company's stock is when you think you know something about that company that others don't. Otherwise, picking stocks at random gives you as good a chance of picking winners as any stock-picking strategy. Never let anyone tell you different."

I had heard all I needed to hear. I had a wad of cash burning a hole in my pocket and I was eager to get in the big-money game of investing. So, with my eyes closed, and chanting, "Eeeny, meeny, miney, mo," I picked my first-ever stock investment. And as dumb luck would have it, just a few months later the small energy company whose stock I purchased at random from the paper that day was acquired at a stock price nearly double what I'd paid. Little did I know at the time that I would go on to spend the greater part of my teen years trying to repeat that initial investing success.

EASY COME, EASY GO

In the months and years that followed that first investment, I would learn that easy money can be as much a curse as a blessing. Perhaps you have heard stories about lottery winners losing their multimillion-dollar fortunes just a few years after hitting the big jackpot. For me it was the same story, just with a smaller pot. I might have had only a few hundred dollars of made money to lose, but that represented all the money I had in the world.

My dad had explicitly warned me not to let "beginner's luck" go to my head. "Lightning," he said, "rarely strikes twice in the same spot." But not surprisingly, being an almost-teenage know-it-all, I wasn't listening to what I didn't want to hear. What did he know, anyway? My dad was a lot of things, but a risk taker was not one of them. Neither he nor my mom believed in shortcuts.

Dad was born and raised in the South Bronx and studied very

hard to earn a full-ride scholarship to Fordham University, where he graduated number one in his class. He then spent twenty-two years as a corporate attorney at JCPenney, where he slowly worked his way up the ladder to become the company's head of litigation, and eventually executive vice president and general counsel of its life insurance division.

My mother received her master's degree in education, and after many years working endless hours as a teacher and school administrator, she became principal of a small Catholic school in a low-income Hispanic neighborhood—an often difficult yet gratifying job she thoroughly enjoyed. The straight-and-narrow path of hard work and patience paid off for both my parents, providing them with the financial means to raise me and my three siblings in upper-class neighborhoods.

Yet, while we were far from poor, my parents were solely reliant on compensation from their careers as a means to building wealth. Investing just wasn't something they did. My dad had a stockbroker only out of necessity, to process the corporate stock grants he occasionally received from his company.

My parents' lack of income diversity made them slaves to their employers. In 1988, when JCPenney suddenly announced it was relocating the company's headquarters from Manhattan to a plot of uninhabited farmland on the border of Texas and Oklahoma, we were left with no other option than to leave our extended family and friends to start a new life two thousand miles away from everything we had ever known. The move tore my large close-knit family in half, both physically and emotionally; we had lived in close proximity for generations.

I was in eighth grade at the time and was forced to change schools mid-year. It was not an easy transition. I was an Italian American kid with a thick "Noo Yawk" accent who had grown up in an ethnic melting pot in the predominantly Jewish neighborhood of Great Neck, Long Island. The people and terrain of Texas were as unfamiliar to me as China would have been.

At that first dreaded cafeteria school lunch west of the Mississippi, I reluctantly took a seat next to a group of my new classmates, some of whom were sporting Field & Stream or Ducks Unlimited baseball caps and chewing tobacco. A note was passed to me from across the table. It read, "Interstate 35 North—Go Home, Yankee."

It would be a full year before I adjusted my wristwatch from Eastern to Central Standard Time. I refused to accept my new life as permanent. I was intent on getting my old life back, and if I could find a shortcut to doing so, all the better. My parents taught us to believe that the fruits of success came only with hard work. But look where all that hard work had gotten us. I might have been only thirteen at the time, but I had tasted the fruits of success in the stock market and I wanted more of it. A lot more! I knew that with enough of it, I could buy my old life back—and never again be at the mercy of others.

WASH AND REPEAT

As a result of that first stock investment, in just a few months I had doubled my savings to nearly $1,000. The stock market would be my ticket out of the hell that was my new life. But I knew it would take a lot more than $1,000 to convince my dad to quit his job and move the family back home to New York. I calculated that if I could just repeat my last investment success and double my $1,000 ten times in a row, I would have a million dollars—easy enough to achieve. So with the newspaper's Business section in hand, eyes closed, I yet again picked a stock at random and proceeded with the next phase of my investment experiment.

I don't remember the name of my second, third, or fourth stock picks. Needless to say, my father was right. That first stock pick had been just blind luck after all. Clearly I couldn't just "will" myself to fortune with wishful thinking. Don't get me wrong. I still believed the stock market to be my golden ticket, but I realized that I would have to step up my investing strategy.

LEARNING THE HARD WAY

I became obsessed. I read all the investing books, and soon knew every *Wall Street Journal* and *Barron's* columnist by name. There wasn't an investment type (stocks, bonds, commodities) or trading strategy (growth, value, momentum) I didn't try.

I recall riding my BMX bike home one summer afternoon from the Dallas commodities exchange while balancing a one-hundred-ounce bar of silver bullion on the handlebars. I had just finished reading a book about the Hunts, one of the world's wealthiest families. They tried to corner the global silver market in the 1970s by amassing more than two hundred million ounces of the metal, equivalent to half the world's deliverable supply.

Unfortunately, my own silver experiment was ultimately more of a novelty than an investment. My $500 silver bar appreciated only $12 in eight months, and if I had held onto it, my investment would have been worth roughly the same amount ten years later. Unless you are seeking an investment that could also serve as the world's most interesting and expensive paperweight, I would leave commodities to the professional speculators.

By the time I turned sixteen, CNBC had become my MTV, and "money honey" finance anchor Maria Bartiromo was my Pamela Anderson. I had become a human sponge for all things financial. If I learned anything worth remembering about investing during those teenage years, it was what drove other people to buy and sell stocks. It was this insight into Wall Street's investing behavior that would eventually empower me to crack the black box of investing success for myself.

2

IF IT'S BROKEN, FIX IT

"The error of the past is the wisdom of the future."
—DALE TURNER

Think of the last car you purchased. Now think about the factors in your decision to purchase that particular car. Was it the car's styling? Or was it passenger capacity, or affordability, or gas mileage, or the number of cup holders? Ask six different people that question and you might get six different answers.

But on Wall Street, two long-established methodologies drive nearly 100 percent of all investment decisions:

1. **Technical analysis:** the study of past market data to forecast the future direction of stock price; and
2. **Fundamental analysis:** the study of the health, financial statements, market, management, and competitors of a company to determine the company's stock value.

Here's what I learned about each:

TECHNICAL ANALYSIS
History Does Not Repeat Itself in Predictable Patterns

If you ever hear someone tell you "the trend is your friend," beware! You are likely listening to someone who has been brainwashed by the pseudoscience that is technical analysis.

I've tried my hand at it—as does nearly every new-to-the-game self-directed investor (as you can judge by the sheer number of investment books that attempt to decipher and promote this age-old investment strategy)—and I found that experimenting with technical analysis is kind of like ordering calf fries (translation for non-Texans: cow testicles) at a restaurant. You know it's a bad idea, but you do it anyway to learn firsthand what you are *not* missing. The legendary self-made billionaire and investor Warren Buffett has said, "I realized technical analysis didn't work when I turned the charts upside down and didn't get a different answer." He also noted, "If past history was all there was to the game, the richest people would be librarians."

Still, the lure of making money simply by observing past peaks and valleys on stock charts is seductive for any potential investor looking to turn a quick profit with minimal effort. Unfortunately, in the case of technical analysis, what seems too good to be true is all too great a temptation for the newbie investor to resist.

The principals of technical analysis have evolved through the observation of financial markets over hundreds of years. Technicians (or "chartists") search to exploit repeatable patterns that are either directly or indirectly related to a stock's price or volume. Technicians purchase stocks that are "trending up" and sell stocks that are "trending down," based on their analysis. Sounds simple, right?

The problem is that stocks, much like the people who buy and sell them, are not as predictable as they appear to be. And when money is at stake, the behavior of crowds trying to profit from the perceived ebb and flow of stock price fluctuations quickly tends to neutralize any price patterns that do exist.

For example, at one time there existed a phenomenon in the stock market known as the "January effect." Every year, more often than not, the stock prices of smaller companies tended to go up more than average during the month of January. The effect is now thought to have been related to end-of-year tax-motivated selling and eventual repurchasing by individual investors.

Once investors began to observe this trend, it disappeared as quickly as it had emerged, because investors sought to purchase stocks ahead of the expected January rise, giving birth to a new phenomenon of buying in the month of December known as the annual "Santa Claus rally." Not surprisingly, as investors chased the Santa Claus rally, it began to appear earlier and earlier in the month, until it, too, evaporated.

As a result of this type of self-correcting market bias, technical trading models have become increasingly cryptic and proprietary over the years, making it more and more difficult for investors on or off Wall Street to keep up with the evolving rules of the so-called science. Conveniently, this serves to protect the perceived value and excessive compensation of the computer engineer voodoo wizards who have become Wall Street's modern-day technical analysts.

Sadly, no matter how many millions are spent and no matter how many MIT computer engineers Wall Street employs to push the limits of technical analysis—Wall Street trading firms now spend countless dollars to employ computers and software that can make millions of trades each *second*, striving for that little edge—the strategy over the long term has proven to be little better than picking stocks at random ("eeny, meeny, miney, mo").

A 322-page study of the field of technical analysis conducted in 2003 by Amsterdam economist Gerwin Griffioen concluded that technical trading for the U.S., Japanese, and Western European stock markets showed no statistically significant forecasting power when you took into account the costs of buying and selling stocks.

Of course, the latest movement in technical analysis leverages computer-assisted techniques to apply complex algorithms in the simulation and decoding of artificial neural networks, completely removing the need for human interpretation of charts. Is your head spinning yet? If Wall Street is great at one thing, it is their ability to repackage, in ways that are indecipherably new and complex, investment strategies proven to be ineffective, to "sell" prospective clients. If we have learned anything from the financial debacle of 2008 it is "garbage in, garbage out." Indeed, now anyone with $299 and a computer can purchase technical charting software off an infomercial that will tell them exactly when to buy and sell nearly any stock in the world.

That's great! As if thirty years of underperformance by overpaid Wall Street technical chartists weren't bad enough, now Uncle Jim Bob can slowly erode the family's retirement savings all by himself, in the comfort of his living room, using the same tea-leaf-reading software as the pros on Wall Street!

Even with the vast amount of published evidence disproving the validity of technical analysis, the super-size interactive charts used by modern-day technical analysts generate too much entertainment value and on-screen color to be ignored by the financial media. Watch any financial news network long enough and you are sure to find a technician lending his or her expertise to providing an interpretation of the day's stock market action. Such analysts have a captivating answer for every question, and those answers are always delivered with absolute confidence. Why did Microsoft's stock go down today? "Well," the analyst will say, "it was clearly coming off a 'head-and-shoulders top' formation and was overdue for a price correction." When asked what a specific stock is going to do tomorrow or next week, the answers become a bit vaguer. Usually the technician will provide two or more possible scenarios in order to produce a technical explanation for any conceivable future price movement. Convenient, right? Technical analysts are perhaps the greatest showmen on Wall Street, and they are highly skilled at masking the shortfalls of their craft. I highly recommend you turn on CNBC or Fox Business and witness their theatrics for yourself. I always find them quite amusing.

As a teenager, I employed a mock trading portfolio to test nearly every technical trading strategy I could get my hands on. You name the strategy, I tested it: double tops, V-tops, Bollinger bands, linear regression, the Elliott wave principle. Rather than using real money, however, I tracked imaginary gains and losses daily by hand, a practice technique that is significantly easier to carry out today by setting up a free virtual trading account through an online broker such as e-Trade or Scottrade. As a result, I never lost any real money—my virtual cash was another story—but I did spend a considerable amount of time (which, as a teenager, I had plenty of). So I was spinning my wheels on technical trading strategies that amounted to little more than smoke and mirrors.

What's the one key takeaway regarding the vast and evolving world of technical analysis? It doesn't work! And if on the off chance one of those Wall Street–hired MIT brainiacs uncovers the crystal ball able to project the future of financial markets on his supercomputer, you can be sure the secret formula won't be sold on infomercials or discussed in books! In the true spirit of Wall Street greed, it will be sold off to the highest-bidding foreign government seeking monetary global dominance.

FUNDAMENTAL ANALYSIS
One Person's Trash Is Another Person's Treasure

What if your family were a publically traded company? It's an interesting concept to ponder. Your family could issue and sell stock to investors that represented a percentage of ownership in its financial future. This would provide you with the ability to raise money without taking on the assumed risk and interest liability of being in debt.

On the downside, you would be forced to share a portion of your family's excess income and future net worth with your investors, and would probably be required to run all family expenses by a board of directors. That's no fun! However, the investment money you received could provide you or members of your family with the resources to pursue a new, more lucrative education path, career, or business venture.

Fundamental analysis involves studying all elements of a company and its financials in order to determine its market value. Let's create a fictional family and see how Wall Street would apply fundamental analysis in formulating that family's stock market value. We'll call our family the Bakers. Drew Baker and his wife, Kara, are both employed and have no children. Drew is a well-paid software engineer, and Kara holds a steady job as a human resources assistant at one of the city's leading interior design firms.

Their combined salary, which we classify as "family revenue," is a healthy $120,000. Unfortunately, the couple plays as hard as they work, spending nearly every dollar of their after-tax family revenue. What little is left every month goes toward paying the high interest fee on nearly $40,000 of credit card debt they have amassed over the years. But all is not lost for the Baker family. Kara has, for many years, demonstrated an eye for interior design, which she pursues as an after-hours and weekend hobby. She has been hired by nearly a dozen of her neighbors to assist with interior design projects, and has even had her design work profiled in the city magazine's Fashion section. Kara, a superb networker, is in all the right social circles—a clear bonus for any aspiring interior designer.

One of the senior partners at the design firm where Kara works has offered her a position as a full-time interior designer with a starting salary nearly triple what she makes as an HR assistant. The sole prerequisite of the offer is that she enroll in school to obtain her degree and certification in interior design. Unfortunately, with tuition running in the tens of thousands of dollars, this is money the Baker family neither has nor can afford to borrow on top of their existing credit card debt.

Like any company, the Baker family generates revenue and incurs expenses. It is not hard to visualize how a small financial investment could provide them with the means to grow their revenue while reducing their debt expense. Unfortunately, public stock markets do not permit families to IPO (meaning Initial Public Offering: that is, bringing a new stock to market) themselves. But if such a market did exist, the Bakers would probably hire an investment banking firm such as Goldman Sachs to help them assess their family value.

If the Bakers were to issue and sell stock representing a 50 percent ownership in their family, they might be able to raise enough money both to send Kara to design school and to pay off their high-interest credit card debt. In that scenario, a debt-free Baker family, with Kara's increased compensation as a designer, might generate $60,000 in excess income after expenses each year. Fifty percent of that amount, or $30,000, would then be distributed to the investor pool annually, in a similar fashion to the way companies distribute their profits as dividends to investors.

How much would that $30,000 annual return be worth to a prospective pool of Baker family investors: $100,000? $250,000? It depends.

It is not uncommon for Wall Street to value some companies at five times their annual profit while valuing others at over forty times their annual profit. Many factors play into that decision. In the case of the Baker family, Wall Street investors would first determine the rate of compensation growth for both Drew's and Kara's jobs, to project how much their $60,000 in excess annual income is likely to grow or shrink over time. The investors would be sure to account for any number of potential risk factors, such as layoffs or health issues, that could potentially impact either of the Bakers' two sources of family revenue. Based on Kara's age, they would probably also calculate the likelihood and associated expenses incurred by the couple should they decide to have children, and the loss of family revenue should Kara or Drew leave their job to raise a child.

Do Drew and Kara have a history of stability in their relationship? A separation or divorce, not to mention the potential legal fees involved, could potentially increase the family's living expenses and spell disaster for their finances.

Having previously buried themselves deep in credit card debt, could the family now be trusted to be fiscally responsible and keep their expenses in check?

How are other families with a similar composition to that of the Baker family being valued in the market?

Do the Bakers even have a long enough financial track record as a family for investors to forecast their financial future accurately?

What's the best-case upside? What's the worst-case downside?

Consider all the possible factors and scenarios that must be probed and evaluated when attempting to place an accurate valuation on the future earnings and expenses of a simple two-person family such as the Bakers.

Now imagine conducting this same exercise for a growing company with hundreds or even thousands of employees, dozens of product lines and competitors around the world. Welcome to the world of investment banking!

With all of the potential scenarios, it should be no surprise that there is no universally accepted way to value a company. Investment bankers weigh many different (and sometimes conflicting) financial ratios to determine a company's value. For any publically traded stock, you might have ten seasoned Wall Street analysts who, after studying the same corporate financials, will provide ten opposing viewpoints on the matter. In the case of the Baker family, a growth-oriented investor might focus on the family's long-term potential to increase revenue by leveraging Kara's design talent, while a value-oriented investor might discount the value of Kara's unknown future earnings potential while placing a higher emphasis on the family's surefire excess income after eliminating their credit card debt and interest expense.

Unlike technical analysis, which uses historical price patterns to predict future price movement, fundamental analysis seeks to find companies with stock prices that are unjustifiably low, based on what is determined to be the company's "true" value. An investor using fundamental analysis to purchase stock believes that he will sell the stock at a higher price once the market recognizes its "mistake" and is willing to pay the stock's "true" value. But if every Wall Street analyst and investor values companies differently based on the financial, growth, and risk assumptions they feel are of the highest importance to them, what does one need in order to trust that the market at large will ever allow the company's stock price to catch up to its hypothetical "true" value?

The answer is patience.

Have you ever taken a liking to an obscure musician, actor, or entertainer who, for whatever reason, was not widely appreciated by the public at large? Maybe they were ahead of their time, had inferior marketing, or just hadn't been given the proper opportunity to shine. You thought, "Someday the rest of the world will recognize this person or band for how great they really are."

I'm not a big underground music fiend, but I do love great independent film. I remember watching a small independent movie in 1996 called *Freeway*, starring an unknown actress who caught my eye. I forced everyone I knew to watch the film, proclaiming that the slightly awkward-looking young actress was destined for superstardom, and would someday win an Academy Award.

My friends and family at the time mostly ignored me, but years later that unknown actress would prove me right by winning an Oscar for her performance opposite Joaquin Phoenix in *Walk the Line*. It actually wasn't all that long before the world took a liking to Reese Witherspoon, but on Wall Street, the smartest person in the room often has to wait years for the rest of the market to catch up to his way of thinking. Just look at the second richest person in the world, investor Warren Buffet, who has said, "If a business does well, the stock eventually follows." But Buffet isn't concerned with how long it takes for the market eventually to recognize the worth of a company he invests in; he is supremely patient and knows that over time a company's profits will demand the respect of the market.

If you think you possess half the patience and financial wit as Warren Buffet, and have the appetite to spend endless hours crunching numbers, contrasting mathematic ratios, and analyzing corporate risk factors, you might try your hand at fundamental analysis. Just know you will be competing with thousands of brilliant MBA-trained business minds. And beware, on the off chance you are able to stand out from the crowd, your time frame for success will more likely be measured in decades than in months or years. If you do have the financial proficiency and temperament to play with the big boys on Wall Street, you might as well work with them and get paid regardless of whether your analysis is correct. Fundamental analysis is a grinding game of inches, and for most of us it is no fun to play.

Here's an important third point:

COMBINING TWO LOSING STRATEGIES DOES NOT RESULT IN A WINNING STRATEGY

I am terrified of flying. It is not a rational fear. I am unable to casually surrender control of my life to airline mechanics. I don't trust pilots I haven't had the opportunity to screen. I carry an emergency smoke hood (aka gas mask) on every flight, in the unlikely event of a cabin fire. (The device, which fits in a canister the size of a soda can, does not make me a friend of TSA agents or of anyone waiting in line behind me at the airport security checkpoint.) I even conduct an analysis of the airline's and aircraft's safety history before I book a flight.

The truth is my paranoia-induced preparation and analysis do little more than provide me with a false sense of control over a situation that is clearly out of my hands. In the same way, Wall Street institutions regularly market their knack for combining the best of technical and fundamental analysis to their clients as part of a balanced investment strategy.

This looks great on paper, but the reality is: an ugly shirt paired with an ugly jacket makes for an ugly outfit. Studies have shown that portfolios managed using an overlapping strategy of technical and fundamental analysis do not perform significantly better over time than portfolios using neither of the two.

Having looked at both schools of thought related to investment analysis, how is one ever to gain an investment edge when buying and selling stocks? Is there a road less traveled, a strategy less accessible to those on Wall Street that we financially inept investing newbies, with limited time and financial proficiency, could use to our benefit?

Let's go back to my fear of flying. You would probably agree that I would have a genuine reason to be fearful if I were to smell alcohol on the pilot's breath, or see black smoke coming from one of the engines prior to takeoff. One way or another, I'm off that plane *now*, even if I have to fake a heart attack—because those factors constitute "game-changing information." I'm betting you'd deplane, too.

Remember the Baker family? What if Wal-Mart chose to test-market a Kara Baker–inspired line of home design accessories at a store in your home town, and after just one month you discovered that the store had nearly sold out of all her products? This is another situation in which you and I would have come into possession of game-changing information. It is not investment analysis, but the art of uncovering game-changing information before others do that is the true Holy Grail of investing.

So if painstaking technical and fundamental analysis have both been exposed as marginally effective at best, why wouldn't every professional on Wall Street be scouring the planet simply to be the first to get ahold of game-changing, stock-moving information?

The answer is simple. Time-honored Wall Street institutions exist and are paid to decipher complex problems they are uniquely qualified to "solve." They make money from selling these professional services, regardless of whether the services make you money. However, the multibillion-dollar Wall Street institutions full of gifted MIT engineers and Harvard-trained financial analysts are ill-equipped to uncover the next fad in video gaming, food, or fashion. Perhaps one day Wall Street will wake up and begin hiring and training behavioral investigators to crack tomorrow's trends, but until then, you can be sure they will busy themselves generating profits by selling what they do best: crunching numbers and analyzing charts. In a financial industry that is richly rewarded for mediocrity, there is simply not enough financial incentive for them to leave their comfort zone. And that is great news for us Wall Street outsiders.

It took me all four years of high school before I realized that I did not have to think like a financial professional to succeed as an investor. That million-dollar fortune I had counted on to be my ticket back to New York hadn't materialized, but as luck would have it, by then I was having the time of my life with people who would become my lifelong friends.

As the years passed, there would be no shortage of motivation for me to make money, and after all of my experimenting, I had the proper mind-set and understanding to succeed. Ironically, it was not trend regression or portable alpha analysis or any other complex-sounding Wall Street toy, but my father's unsophisticated advice, "buy when you know something that others don't," that would go on to lay the groundwork for my greatest stock picks and would define my future success as an investor—thus proving that sometimes the simplest answers are indeed the truest.

3

NOBODY KNOWS ANYTHING

Zoning Out the Financial "Experts" and "Professionals"

Meet Jack Grubman. As Salomon Smith Barney's top telecom analyst, he earned compensation of $20 million a year. Grubman, who received an MS in mathematical statistics from Columbia University, has been profiled by the *Wall Street Journal*, *BusinessWeek*, and even *New York* magazine.

In March of 2001, Grubman issued a twenty-eight-page report that proclaimed, "Over the next 12 to 18 months, investors will look back at current prices of the leading players and wish that they had bought stock at these prices."[1] Of the ten companies he picked, just a year later, five went on to trade below $1 a share. Three of those five filed for bankruptcy.

Analysis conducted by MarketPerform.com for CNNMoney.com shows that if you had acted on each of Grubman's "buy" recommendations since February 1999 and sold when he downgraded the stock, you would have suffered a 74.5 percent loss.

In October of 2001, Jack Grubman lost his crown as Institutional Investor's number-one wire line services analyst—but amazingly kept his job as an analyst for Salomon Smith Barney for a short period of time, where his stock picks continued to be shared with millions of clients through the firm's thirteen thousand brokers.

There are two jobs most of us would drool to have: Wall Street analyst and Los Angeles or Las Vegas TV weatherman (". . . and tomorrow, another sunny day!"). These are two jobs in which you can be utterly useless, yet be paid handsomely, so long as you look and sound good.[2]

William Goldman, the American novelist, playwright, and two-time Academy Award–winning screenwriter, wrote, "The single most important fact, perhaps, of the entire movie industry: Nobody knows anything. . . . Not one person in the entire motion picture field *knows* for a certainty what's going to work. Every time out it's a guess—and, if you're lucky, an educated one."[3]

I can't say for sure whether those words speak absolute truth in Hollywood, but they couldn't be a more accurate depiction of Wall Street, where the story of Jack Grubman is far from an anomaly. Even with billions of dollars at stake, access to the brightest MBA-grad minds, and nearly a century of accumulated investment expertise, the average professionally managed stock fund returns roughly 2 percent less per year to its shareholders than the stock market returns in general.[4]

Imagine a casino where every gambler paid a commissioned professional to determine which slots to pull, or whether to put roulette chips on red or black. Seems ludicrous, right? Equally unthinkable would be paying fees to a middleman to assist you in picking lottery ticket numbers. This is because we compensate others for providing us with transparent and equitable value—be it a product or service.

At least with respect to the aforementioned games of chance, a professional middleman can statistically do no worse than you could do yourself, meaning the harm inflicted on your wallet would be limited to his fees and commissions.

Professionally managed investment funds and portfolios, on the other hand, by adding the deeply flawed human element of stock analysis, actually perform worse on average than an equally weighted basket of random stocks—meaning you pay for the privilege of making less money.

Over the five-year period from 2004 through 2008, investing in the S&P 500, a weighted index of five hundred of the largest public companies in the United States—an investment that anyone can make while paying virtually zero fees—would have made you more money than 72 percent of professionally managed large-cap mutual funds, whose sole job it is to handpick (for a fee) specific S&P 500 large company stocks that they believe are likely to perform best.[5]

The S&P MidCap 400 index, which consists of an equal weighting of four hundred mid-size public companies in the United States, outperformed 76 percent of professionally managed funds investing in mid-size companies; and the S&P SmallCap 600 index, which consists of an equal weighting of six hundred small-size public companies in the United States, outperformed 86 percent of professionally managed funds investing in small-size companies.[6]

These results are similar to that of the previous five-year cycle from 1999 through 2003, according to results from Standard & Poor's Indices Versus Active Funds Scorecard. Published research shows similar results for international stock and bond funds.

Even the age-old perception that professional money managers are able to preserve wealth through bad economic times has proven to be nothing more than a sham. "The belief that bear [downward trending] markets strongly favor active [professional] management is a myth," says Srikant Dash, global head of research and design at Standard & Poor's. "A majority of active funds regardless of fund type (aggressive growth, value, income, etc.) were outperformed by indices during the down markets of 2008."[7] The bear market of 2000 through 2002 showed similar outcomes. Case in point: during the worldwide economic collapse of 2008, Harvard, the world's richest university, with infinite access to financial intelligence and talent, lost $11 billion of its $37 billion endowment, a professionally managed portfolio that the school depends on to fund about 35 percent of its operating budget. Some of Harvard's degree programs rely on the school's endowment fund income to cover more than 50 percent of their expenses.

As cost-cutting measures, the school chose to scale back on hot breakfasts in most dorms, retract its free sweatsuit policy for certain varsity athletes, and ask professors to go without cookies at faculty meetings. One would think a more appropriate cost-cutting action would have been to trim the school's curriculum related to the study of financial markets or at least downsize its staff of financial advisers.

How is it possible that Wall Street's smartest minds, with unlimited resources at their disposal, could be so bad at the one thing they get paid to do well? These are career financial "experts" with Ivy League educations making millions at Wall Street's most prestigious firms. Could they really all just be bad stock pickers? And if such is the case, how did a financial profession so entrenched in underperformance gain such a stranglehold over us investors, who are savvy shoppers with respect to other areas of our lives? After all, without our hard-earned money, the Wall Street middleman would cease to exist.

A BRIEF HISTORY OF THE PROFESSIONAL STOCK PICKER

You wouldn't think twice about having anyone other than a board-certified surgeon operate on you or a family member, and should you ever find yourself entangled in a civil or criminal suit, chances are you would hire the best attorney you could afford. In these situations, it is clear that the specialized knowledge and skills of an educated medical or legal professional would increase your likelihood of a positive outcome.

While we hope never to need their services, surgeons and attorneys have proven their value over many centuries. People have been studying medicine since the beginning of the seventh century in ancient Arabia, and the origins of focused schooling in law date back to the Islamic madrasahs (educational institutions) from the ninth century.

The academic study of financial markets, however, proves to have a much briefer history. While the Dutch East India Company became the world's first publicly traded company in 1602, the world's first business school, the École Supérieure de Commerce de Paris (now ESCP Europe), wasn't founded until 1819, less than two hundred years ago. The postgraduate study of modern financial markets didn't begin until the formation of the University of Pennsylvania's Wharton School of Business in 1881, at the cusp of what would become an American-fueled revolution in financial analysis and investment management.

A glimpse into Wall Street circa 1900 would reveal a primitive and unregulated industry comprising robber barons and all-powerful bankers, insurers, and professional trustees. Lack of market and government oversight contributed to a Wild West mentality on the Street, where conflicts of interest among investment professionals ran rampant.

For decades a small number of mega-powerful financial tycoons acted as the sole gatekeepers to American capital markets. They dictated investment decisions for their clients, often directing their funds into high-risk, closely held financing projects with the primary goal of lining their own pockets. Abuses of power were accepted as an evil but necessary by-product of fast-moving industrial progress.

One of the most famous of the early tycoons, J.P. Morgan, is known to have financed the purchase of antiquated rifles being sold by the U.S. Army for $3.50 each. Morgan's partner re-machined the rifles and sold them back to the army for $33.00 each. The guns were later found to be defective, at times blowing the thumbs off the men who used them.[8] (J.P. Morgan, like many wealthy persons of that era, avoided military service altogether, by paying $300 for a military substitute.) The story, as outlandish as it seems today, was indicative of the routine abuses of power among the robber barons that had become commonplace by the end of the nineteenth century.

In an attempt to curb such abuses, "in 1912, Arsène Pujo, a Democratic congressman from Louisiana, received authorization to form a House committee to investigate the 'money trust'," a small group of Wall Street bankers.[9] The committee exposed the bankers as having overtly abused the public's trust by exerting their influence and control over the nation's finances. This inspired public support for ratification in 1913 of the Sixteenth Amendment, which authorized a national income tax. This tax would stimulate consumer investing in the years ahead, as wealthy Americans sought to find ways to replace that lost income with investment gains.

A few years later America would go on to issue war bonds, also called liberty loans. By 1919 more than eleven million patriotic Americans had invested in liberty loans, many of which were marketed and purchased through Wall Street financial institutions such as J.P. Morgan and Merrill Lynch. These firms quickly found themselves with an opportunity to initiate client relationships with millions of wide-eyed Americans with aspirations to the middle class but zero investing experience.

In the 1920s, America was for the first time starting to develop an appetite for investing. However, investing in U.S. companies was still viewed as a highly precarious and risky activity. According to pioneering investment adviser Theodore T. Scudder, "Corporate morals were so low that common stocks of practically all publicly held companies could be considered nothing more than outright speculations."[10]

The pump was primed. The enticement of new wealth, combined with a volatile stock market and a tsunami of eager first-time investors with little business education or knowledge of financial markets, set the stage for what would grow to become the largest and most financially lucrative industry of middlemen the world has ever seen.

Over the coming decades, the Wharton School of Business and others that followed its lead would supply a blooming industry of self-anointed stock-picking experts who—working under the guise of professional financial analysts, advisers, and fund managers—would skim trillions of dollars in fees from the world economy without any proof of having provided value to their clients' finances beyond that of statistical chance. In less than a century, a budding financial services profession would engrain itself into every aspect of modern American society, where it now generates an astonishing $1 trillion plus in fees every year, which represents more than 2.5 percent of the country's total financial assets.

So what does Wall Street do with all that money? As it turns out, stocks are not the only item for which financial professionals tend to overpay. In early 2008, Merrill Lynch CEO John A. Thain, a former Goldman Sachs executive who once headed the New York Stock Exchange, spent more than $1.22 million of the firm's money to freshen up his personal office suite. According to CNBC, the list of items brought in for Mr. Thain's office suite remodel, and their cost, was as follows:

Area rug	$87,784
Mahogany pedestal table	$25,713
Nineteenth-century credenza	$68,179
Pendant light furniture	$19,751
Four pairs of curtains	$28,091
Pair of guest chairs	$87,784
George IV chair	$18,468
Six wall sconces	$2,741
Parchment wastecan	$1,405
Roman shade fabric	$10,967
Roman shades	$7,315
Coffee table	$5,852
Commode on legs	$35,115

According to documents, a whopping $800,000 of the $1.22 million spent went to compensate renowned interior designer Michael S. Smith, whose celebrity client list includes Steven Spielberg, Michelle Pfeiffer, Cindy Crawford, and Michelle Obama. The frivolous use of corporate cash looks even more excessive when one learns that the White House, which has a notorious reputation for overpaying vendors, paid Smith only $100,000 for his interior design services—for what we have to assume was a larger job than Thain's Manhattan office suite.

Such stories of modern-day Wall Street excess would not be

possible were it not for the "productization" (i.e., the packaging and marketing of conceptual investment strategies as mass-market consumer products) of financial markets. It was government-sanctioned war bonds that gave ordinary Americans their first taste of investing in the early twentieth century, and during the latter half of the century it was the unintended consequences of another government-engineered investment program that fueled the mass consumer adoption of "investment products" in America.

THE 401(K) PLAN
Wall Street's Gateway Drug

In 1978, Congress amended the Internal Revenue Code by adding section 401(k), whereby employees are not taxed on income they choose to receive as deferred compensation as part of a company-sponsored retirement plan. The law went into effect on January 1, 1980, and by 2003 there were 438,000 U.S. companies with 401(k) plans. Thanks in large part to the 401(k), today over 52 percent of households in the United States own a mutual fund, with many of those households having made their very first investment through their company-sponsored 401(k) retirement plan.

Spend more than five minutes listening to Dave Ramsey, Suze Orman, Jean Chatzky, or any of the other practical money advice authorities, and chances are you will hear them preaching the value of the 401(k) as one of the best places to put your money—that is, of course, after you've paid down all your credit card debt. For most people, most of the time, this advice is absolutely correct—which, ironically, is unfortunate for all of us.

Like most mid- to large-size American companies, my former

employer offered a company-sponsored 401(k) retirement plan, to which I had made monthly contributions for nine years. Each month, my company matched a percentage of what I contributed to the plan— a feature unique to company-sponsored 401(k) plans. Unlike the investments that sit outside my retirement account, my 401(k) plan allows me to invest pre-tax dollars, while delaying for decades payment of all taxes—even those on stock gains I amass over time—until I begin to withdraw money from the 401(k), ideally during my retirement years, when I'm at a lower income tax bracket.

The combined benefits of company matching and tax deferrals make the 401(k) a winning investment vehicle—with one colossal exception. As is commonplace with nearly all company-sponsored retirement plans, investment options for employees contributing money to their 401(k) are more often than not confined to a handful of fee-based mutual funds chosen by an investment firm contracted by the company to be the 401(k) plan's adviser. The investment firm that successfully sells its way into your employer's human resources or finance department to become the company's 401(k) plan adviser enjoys a captive audience of clients, including you and all of your coworkers. This ability to handcuff an entire organization and its employees makes the 401(k) one of the most financially lucrative investment vehicles for a financial institution involved in fee-based investment management.

The plan at my company allowed us to choose from among nine mutual fund options. Each was marketed as a "no load" fund, meaning it charged zero upfront commission—when in actuality it extracted recurring annual expense fees, known as "soft fees," of 1 to 3 percent. Over a thirty-year period, a recurring annual expense fee of just 2 percent can reduce the value of your retirement portfolio by more than 50 percent. These recurring fees, which are often explained in the funds' marketing material in obscure language that is difficult for the amateur investor to understand, are the dirty little secret of the mutual fund industry.

Unlike "hard" upfront commissions, "soft" expense fees are not billed to the investor but instead are deducted annually from the fund's combined pool of investment money. A $100 million fund with a "soft" 2 percent expense fee that generates an 8 percent annual investment return will simply deduct its $2 million in fees from its $8 million in investment gains, reporting to you a return of only 6 percent on your investment, not the 8 percent the fund's portfolio of investments actually made. Likewise, if the fund loses 8 percent, it will tack on its $2 million in fees to its $8 million investment loss. Say you invested $10,000 in the fund. Your statement will simply show a 10 percent, or $1,000, annual loss, when in actuality 25 percent, or $250, of that $1,000 loss is due to the fund's expense fees.

The problem with "soft" expense fees is that they are not separated out for you on your account statements. Unless you do your own math, you have no way of knowing how much you are actually paying.

Nearly all of the expertly managed funds comprising my retirement portfolio underperformed the stock market over the nine years I made 401(k) contributions. For this underperformance, I had the privilege of paying nearly $20,000 in fund management fees, a calculation I was left to do on my own. Ironically, this $20,000 in fees happened to be nearly the same amount of money that my employer contributed to my 401(k) plan in matching funds over the years. Over time, the compounding effect of mutual fund fees can neutralize much if not all of the benefits of even the best-intentioned corporate 401(k) programs.

Even so, the 401(k) is more popular today than it ever has been. Roughly fifty million working Americans have 401(k)-style plans.

The median 401(k) account balance is now about $23,000. By applying an industry median 1 percent annual fund expense fee, we are able to estimate fees generated solely from company-sponsored 401(k) plan contributions to be $11.5 billion (i.e., 50,000,000 × $23,000 × 1 percent).

Even more astonishing is the negative impact on our retirement account that the $11.5 billion in fees buys us investors. By returning roughly 2 percent less per year to shareholders than the stock market returns, the professional money managers cost our retirement accounts $23 billion every year (i.e., 50,000,000 × $23,000 × 2 percent). Those numbers go up nearly tenfold when you include the nearly $10 trillion in mutual fund investments held by investors outside of retirement accounts—not to mention the countless billions paid in "hard" fund commissions. Try to think of any other industry that gets away with being paid tens of billions of dollars to lose hundreds of billions of dollars for their clients, consistently, year after year, unquestioned.

In testimony to Congress, former senator Peter G. Fitzgerald (R-Ill.), chairman of the Senate Subcommittee on Financial Management, referred to the $7 trillion U.S. mutual fund industry as "the world's largest skimming operation." A politician may never have spoken truer words.

From the Roaring Twenties to the mid-twentieth-century Golden Era of American capitalism to the more recent technology and dot-com booms, the behavioral effects of fear, specifically the form of fear known as greed (defined as the "fear of lack"), enabled an industry of sharply dressed, well-spoken professionals with advanced educational degrees and pseudo stock-picking expertise to benefit at the expense of financially intimidated Americans terrified of not participating in their generation's era of financial prosperity.

Even so, the financial advisers, analysts, and fund managers who have proven themselves statistically ineffective as stock pickers are as much an innocent by-product of the financial industry's institutional conflicts of interest and deeply flawed methodologies as are we naïve investors. More often than not, they are hardworking people who spend their days examining financial statements and mountains of data to the best of their ability on behalf of their firms' clients. They never realize that the very education, training, and left-brain mind-set that uniquely qualify them to be high-paid financial professionals are what actually hinder their ability to succeed as stock pickers.

BLESSING IN DISGUISE
How I Narrowly Escaped a Career of Mediocrity on Wall Street

Since my first stock trade at age twelve, I dreamed of someday working one of those Wall Street jobs where I could pick stocks for a living. It was my destiny—or so I thought.

I likely never would have seen the inside of a brokerage house if it hadn't been for Michael Crockett. Crockett and I were roommates and the best of friends at SMU, a private southern university known for its high concentration of trust-fund kids. Crockett, a working student on a full-ride scholarship, was definitely not one of them. Having grown up in a small West Texas desert town, he was crude yet wicked smart— a tobacco-chewing, Texas State debate champion who thought it completely acceptable to use our bedroom carpet as a depository for his tobacco spit.

During our junior year at SMU, Crockett helped me land my first "suit and tie" job, working alongside him as a sales intern at Dean

Witter Investments (now part of Morgan Stanley), where we turned cold calls into warm leads for the firm's senior brokers. It was a miserable job.

As interns, every afternoon, after school and before work, we'd cruise the streets of nearby neighborhoods marking down addresses of houses that had new model cars in their driveways. While not entirely reliable, the presence of a new model car was an easy-to-spot indicator of a family's financial well-being. Using the firm's reverse address listing book, we would look up the names and phone numbers for each address.

On a good shift, I might complete fifty cold calls to convert just one warm lead. Crockett, on the other hand, would consistently convert one out of every two cold calls he made. It was startling to watch. Whether the person he was calling was a potato farmer, computer engineer, or retired war veteran, Crockett had the ability to connect personally with every prospect willing to pick up the phone. If there'd been a Michael Jordan of cold-calling, it would have been Crockett.

It didn't take me long to grasp what little value the firm placed on stock picking. Above all, we were a sales and marketing organization. In fact, there was very little stock picking being done by any of the firm's successful brokers. Everyone had his or her place in the firm's finely tuned money-making hierarchy.

We interns and sales trainees developed warm leads for the brokers. The brokers turned those warm leads into new client accounts for their branch office. The lion's share of funds deposited by those clients was then placed into "managed money" accounts, managed by the executive fund managers who served as "expert" stock pickers at the firm's Wall Street headquarters.

That is where I wanted to be—though it would not be I, but Crockett, who went on to fulfill that dream, while attending Wall Street's most prestigious training program at Goldman Sachs. I would get my fair share of training as a stock picker, though it would be a great deal less conventional and it would take place far from Wall Street. The investing instincts I developed over time would not be influenced by investment experts and professionals under the guise of aptitude and experience. And that was okay, as I was fortunate to learn early on that, as in Hollywood, on Wall Street, "no one knows anything."

4

OTHER PEOPLE'S MONEY

Trading a Life of Financial Mediocrity for
Financial Prosperity

"Often the difference between a successful person and
a failure is not one's better abilities or ideas, but the courage that one
has to bet on one's ideas, to take a calculated risk—and to act."
—ANDRÉ MALRAUX, FRENCH HISTORIAN

Suppose that you are the only income earner in the family, and you have a good job guaranteed to give you (and your family) income every year for life. You are given the opportunity to take a new and equally good job, with a fifty-fifty chance it will double your (family) income and a fifty-fifty chance that it will cut it by a third. Would you take the new job?

This question was posed as part of a 1995 University of Michigan study to measure risk aversion by gauging respondents' willingness to gamble on lifetime income. The results show most of the population declining to take the risk, despite its having a clear monetary advantage in their favor.

The experiment was one of many conducted over the past several decades, all of which show that when offered an even-odds gamble between winning a relatively large amount of money and losing a relatively small amount of money, most people will refuse the bet. Only when the size of the reward is more than twice the size of the potential loss do people decide that the risk is worth taking. This is because people fear losing money, often to the point of irrationality. The more money at stake, the more likely we are to exhibit extreme risk-averse behavior.

British scientists recently used MRI scans to analyze the brains of people playing gambling games. They discovered that losing, or even anticipating the loss of money, stimulates a person's striatum, the part of the brain circuitry that processes fear and pain. This cause-and-effect relationship serves to help the brain guard itself against perceived harm, just as it does when presented with imminent physical injury.

More recent research spearheaded by neuroscientists at the California Institute of Technology shows patients with damaged amygdala—the almond-shaped groups of nuclei within the brain's striatum—demonstrate uncommon risk-tolerant traits. During experimental games of chance, those with damaged amygdala were far more willing than the other group to take rational financial risks such as a fifty-fifty gamble on winning $20 or losing $15—a risk most people will reject, in spite of the positive net expected outcome. (If you lose once and win once, you're still up $5.)

For investors, the hard-wired human aversion to losing money presents a considerable psychological barrier to overcome, because the sole path to successful investing, regardless of one's methods or beliefs, is to risk loss. The Russians have a saying: "He who doesn't risk never gets to drink champagne." The problem is that most people don't believe they can afford to take on financial risk. This is where the ultra wealthy hold a unique advantage, as their worries associated with taking moderate financial risks are reduced.

Let's go back to the University of Michigan's study on willingness to gamble on lifetime income. It turns out that risk tolerance rose at the very high end of the wealth distribution, because high-wealth individuals are thought to have interpreted the survey questions differently from other respondents. Because labor income for a high-net-worth individual is a smaller fraction of that person's total financial resources, this class of society can regularly afford to take chances to their financial benefit. A person with a net worth of $3 million is more likely to risk 20 percent of his $100,000 annual salary ($20,000) on an aggressive investment opportunity than a person with a net worth of $300,000 who earns the same $100,000 annual salary. Thus the rich continually set themselves up to become even richer, while the rest of us—who are rightfully hesitant to take on even calculated risks of size due to the possibility of endangering our (family's) financial security—are stuck in a catch-22 situation, forever pursuing the financial prosperity that itself often serves as a prerequisite to achieving financial prosperity in the first place.

Those individuals who are not able to achieve their desired level of wealth through career success, inheritance, or luck are often destined to live a life of financial mediocrity. And while it has been proven possible for nearly anyone to amass wealth through disciplined, diversified investing over many decades, the sad truth is that most of us have neither the time nor the patience required to slowly grow old rich—or, at least we prefer for that not to be our only path for achieving our financial goals in life.

If only there were a way to bypass the psychological fear of losing money, to find the will to pursue high-reward investments while being confident that such actions will have zero affect on your family savings, financial security, and ability to invest for retirement. Who hasn't said to himself, "If I had only invested in that company" or "If I had only been in a position in life to jump on that opportunity"?

To live without financial regret is a luxury typically enjoyed only by a privileged few who sit at the highest end of the wealth spectrum. But it doesn't need to be that way. Every person, regardless of his financial health or place in life, can position himself to achieve personal financial freedom—whether that means generating $100,000 or $1,000,000—within a reasonable time frame measured not in decades but in months and years.

For the remainder of this book, I will demonstrate precisely how I did just that, in my spare time, while working a full-time job, using in part money I never even knew I had.

OTHER PEOPLE'S MONEY

Ralph Waldo Emerson said, "I dip my pen in the blackest ink, because I'm not afraid of falling into my inkpot." Emerson, perhaps one of the boldest and most outspoken of the great American philosophers and essayists, was not afraid to take chances with his words. Likewise, those who have prospered most on Wall Street have all shared one important trait, enabling them to take unprecedented chances with money.

Be it the financial robber barons of the early twentieth century or the loathed modern-day derivative traders dealing in mortgage-backed securities, those who have amassed the largest fortunes on Wall Street have all done so by leveraging other people's money— money belonging to their clients and investors, people like you and me. Doing so enabled them to take bold risks at our expense on high-stakes investments with big potential payoffs, in which they personally had everything to gain and very little to lose.

It became clear to me early in life that to achieve my financial goals in a timely fashion, I, too, would have to find the courage and resources to bet and bet big on my own investing ideas. So I created my own investing "inkpot" of sorts—a virtual subaccount within my investing accounts, where I could fearlessly invest with conviction, funded exclusively with money I wasn't afraid to lose, money I never intended to have in the first place, money I could leverage and reinvest many times over to turn hundreds of dollars into thousands, and thousands into millions.

I refer to this as my Big Money account. And emulating those on Wall Street, I label all of the money used to fund my Big Money investments OPM, short for Other People's Money. Yet unlike on Wall Street, the OPM funds that comprise my Big Money account do not belong to anyone other than me.

OPM is money that under normal circumstances you would spend, but instead choose to save due to its future potential investment value.

Whether clipping coupons or instituting negligible lifestyle trade-offs such as brewing my morning coffee at home or washing my own car, I turn small amounts of "newfound" money, perceived to be insignificant amounts, into smoldering embers of investment capital. Trivial dollars once casually doled out to Starbucks and the local carwash ignite and fuel my multimillion-dollar Big Money investing account.

The goal of a Big Money account is simple: turn every $1 of OPM into $100. This seemingly far-fetched goal is surprisingly achievable with as little as one winning investment every one to two years. The trick is learning how to pick that one winning investment and understanding how to apply some very simple tools of financial leverage. (We'll talk about these later.)

First, we need to find the money to invest. Even when money is tight, it is possible. The trick to "finding" money in your budget is to evaluate cash not at its current worth, but at its potential worth as a Big Money investor. Before long, you will begin to see a $1 not for its par $1 value but for its $100 maximum investment potential. In doing so, you will open up a whole new world of possibilities—one in which you will become inspired to uncover new, increasingly large sources of OPM from every aspect of your life.

For example, for years my wife and I have kept a running list of items we each want but don't necessarily need. As our budget permits, we buy the items off our list, switching between stuff she wants, stuff I want, and stuff we both want. A few years ago I added a sixty-seven-inch HDTV to the list, at a cost of $2,000. But when the time came for me to buy that TV, I hesitated to pull the trigger. Prices of HDTVs were only going down, and I knew that delaying the purchase could save me hundreds of dollars—money that could go into my Big Money account.

The dilemma was, I watch a lot of television, and once you have experienced watching an action film or sporting event on a large-screen HDTV, it is really hard to enjoy doing so any other way. A few hundred dollars in itself just wasn't enough of a financial trade-off for me to accept the lifestyle sacrifice—in other words, a couple of hundred dollars wasn't enough of an incentive for me to live without an HDTV. That was until I took into consideration the maximum investment potential of those few hundred dollars. When multiplied by a factor of one hundred, that $100 became $10,000.

With this new number in mind, the next fall and winter I proceeded to spend nearly every Sunday watching football at the houses of generous friends with HDTVs. It wasn't until a year later that I purchased—for $1,600—the same sixty-seven-inch Samsung TV I had my heart set on buying the previous year for $2,000. I ultimately got the TV I wanted, but more important, I got to deposit $400, the difference between what I paid and what I originally budgeted, into my Big Money investing account. It wasn't the $400 but rather the future prospect of turning that $400 into $40,000 that inspired me to delay my HDTV purchase.

Each of us has a limit on financial frugality and sacrifice—an unspoken line in the sand where personal financial gain does not warrant the perceived effort expended to pursue such gain. That line is where your everyday savings intentions end and the opportunity to use the 100× money multiplier to accumulate Other People's Money for your Big Money investing account begins. When it comes to instituting behavioral change, Benjamin Franklin can be far more convincing than George Washington.

A recent University of Florida study tracked the eye movements of pool players during the execution of a shot. Those players whose eyes were fixated longest on the target—rather than on the ball being hit—were most successful at executing the shot. It has been argued that this correlation between target-oriented eye fixation and performance success plays out in other sports, such as golf.

Applying this logic to behavior related to earning, saving, and spending money would have you focus away from the value of money in its current form to seeing it for its maximum future potential, the target. No different from successful athletes, those people with a knack for creating wealth for themselves consistently keep their eyes on the prize.

As a mental exercise, apply the 100× money multiplier to all existing and prospective financial transactions in your life, and you will be amazed at how much hidden money you are able to uncover every month. You might consider joining a carpool for gas savings or begin brown-bagging lunches.

This "new to you" money that you are able to save or earn as a result of viewing money for its maximum potential is the money you will designate in your life and financial accounts as OPM. For example, let's say you currently get your haircut every four weeks. If the potential maximum investment value of haircut savings (when calculated using the 100× money multiplier) inspires you to extend your appointments out to every six weeks, or to begin cutting or coloring your own hair from home, those incremental dollars saved (money that would ordinarily have been handed over to your hair salon back when you viewed a dollar as $1) will be designated as OPM and deposited into your Big Money investing account.

Do you dread negotiating with car dealers, traveling off-peak hours, buying groceries in bulk, or comparison shopping on- and offline to save a few dollars? If the potential savings weren't worth the emotional hassle before, they just might be now after you apply the 100× money multiplier. Buy generic products, bottle your own water, mow your own grass, postpone big purchases, and haggle. Most important, think of these new acts of thriftiness not as trivial achievements in how to "live on less" but as exciting new sources of OPM to be used toward investing in the life you've always wanted.

MY FAVORITE SOURCE OF OPM

Former vice president Al Gore coined the term *lockbox,* a protected fund of taxpayer cash to be used exclusively for safekeeping and ensuring future Social Security distributions. While many debate whether the government should be keeping a lockbox of money on our behalf, few would argue that all of us, regardless of our age, should maintain and regularly contribute money to our own hypothetical lockbox—whether it exists in the form of a savings account, a well-diversified retirement investment account, or equity in our home.

This is the money that will serve to ensure your and your family's financial security now and in the future. As important as it may be, nowhere in this book will I attempt to design a financial model for your lockbox—as there are thousands of qualified financial planners and an abundance of great financial planning books and resources across the Internet to help you determine the right mix of age-appropriate financial products for your lockbox. Also, lockbox investing can be incredibly boring to read about, and even more boring to write about—with the one exception being when your lockbox has the potential to serve as a source of OPM.

MY LOCKBOX STORY

For years I had looked forward to this day. After nearly a decade of working for my employer, I had submitted my resignation. Over the prior three-year period, my stock market investments had generated income that far exceeded that from my day job, allowing me to build up a sizable seven-figure nest egg—a feat I would never have dreamed possible just a few years earlier, considering the size of my then-modest stock portfolio.

As a thirty-five-year-old retiree, I was off to author a book about my success as a self-directed investor. It was an exciting time in my life. And to top it off, my wife and I were just weeks away from becoming first-time parents—of twins, no less. Yet despite all of the extraordinary personal and business ventures unfolding, I chose to spend the entirety of my employer's exit interview jubilantly gloating to my HR manager about the newfound freedom I now had as a departing employee to transfer the contents of my company-sponsored 401(k) account (which over the years had grown to $130,000) into a self-managed retirement account at my online broker, Scottrade.

I could barely contain my excitement. I would soon forever leave the world of "actively managed" fee-based investment products imposed on me by my company's 401(k) plan adviser in favor of the "suit killer" of all investments products: the exchange-traded index fund.

Professionally managed mutual funds set out, most often unsuccessfully (as we have learned), to outperform market indexes by hand-picking for a fee what the fund manager perceives to be the "best stocks" within a defined index (company size, geographic location, industry category). Exchange-traded index funds, however, set out simply to replicate the performance of a defined stock market index by holding in its portfolio every stock listed in the index or a representative sample of the stocks in the index.

This is a job mostly managed by a computer. Consequently, index funds do not require an expensive staff of financial analysts and technical engineers, and this results in fund expense savings as high as 95 percent. Those savings are passed along to the investor in the form of dramatically lower fund expense fees. According to the Government Accountability Office, a one-percentage-point decrease in fees would increase retirement income by almost 20 percent after twenty years and 30 percent over thirty years.

The index fund I rolled my retirement funds into was structured to mirror the performance of the S&P 500. The annual management and marketing fee charged by the index fund? Just two tenths of

1 percent. When compared to the near 2 percent annual fee charged by the professionally managed mutual fund in my old 401(k) plan, this meant I would be saving $2,340 a year in fund fees.

And that's not even the best part. Statistically, my S&P 500 index fund was 72 percent more likely to outperform the professionally managed S&P 500 mutual fund held by my old 401(k). Study after study has shown that investors have done no better with the average mutual fund than they could have done by holding an unmanaged broad index of stocks by purchasing a low-fee index fund.

Midway through my exit interview, I became aware of how odd I must have seemed preaching and obsessing over the cost efficiency of my now ex-company's financial retirement plan products. So I tried to justify my level of enthusiasm to Jamie, the HR manager administering the exit interview, in a way to which she could relate.

As a time-stricken single professional with a take-charge attitude toward her career and personal life, Jamie, who happened also to be a good friend of mine, occasionally employed the services of an online dating company. I asked her to imagine a world in which her employment with the company prohibited her from using her preferred online dating service. Instead, she would be restricted to choosing one of a handful of local professional matchmakers contracted by the company. The professional matchmakers all charged exorbitant fees in the thousands of dollars—many times what her online dating service charged—money that Jamie would have to pull directly from her designer clothing budget. And her pool of dating candidates, once in the millions, would now be limited to a small number of handpicked clients influenced by the taste and preferences of a self-proclaimed matchmaking professional.

Jamie, who was by now hanging on my every word, interjected, "I'd die single before doling out a dime of my hard-earned shopping budget to a professional love broker!" At that moment I knew she had seen the light. I responded, "And I'd go broke before taking another job at a company that contracted with incompetent pseudo-professionals to skim money from my hard-earned retirement savings."

The $2,340 I was to save each year in mutual fund fees meant something much greater to me than Jamie could ever realize. Those savings, when multiplied by one hundred, played a large role in prompting my decision to leave the company, as from that point on I would designate each of those saved dollars as OPM for funding future Big Money investments.

Should you ever find yourself trapped in a restrictive company-sponsored 401(k) plan with limited high-fee investment options, *do not quit your job*. But do join forces with your colleagues and demand that your company's plan administrator add a low-fee exchange-traded index fund option to the plan. Over time, the compounded cost savings generated through reduced management fees will greatly increase the value of your lockbox account. And if the annual cost savings don't seem worth the stress of assembling a confrontational coup d'état with your benefits administrator, multiply those annual savings by one hundred and reassess your willingness to champion change for your organization. If you are successful in your efforts, you might just have found yourself a significant new source of recurring OPM funds—and there is no sweeter form of Other People's Money than that which is taken directly from the pockets of Wall Street fat cats.

COMPARTMENTALIZING INVESTMENT RISKS

Financial gain and financial risk always go hand in hand. You can never fully eliminate the element of risk in investing, but thanks to your newfound knack for uncovering OPM for funding Big Money investments, you now have the resources and means to compartmentalize investment risk.

On one hand, you have your lockbox account, a relatively risk-averse pool of money to which you make regular contributions with a goal of providing long-term financial security for you and your family. In a single afternoon, leveraging free financial educational resources on the Internet, I designed lockbox investment plans for both myself and my parents. My lockbox is comprised of low-fee domestic and international exchange-traded index funds, whereas my parents' lockbox is comprised mostly of cash and bank CDs. As I age, my lockbox investment allocation will likely begin to look more and more like that of my parents.

On the other hand, you have your Big Money account—a risk-tolerant pool of Other People's Money that is leveraged and invested to provide you and your family with the opportunity to reach your desired financial goals within a concise time frame. Unlike the conservative, well-diversified investments in my lockbox account, it is not unusual for over 50 percent of my Big Money account to be invested in a single company. My parents are nearly twice my age, yet their Big Money account profile is identical to mine.

Your lockbox ensures your financial security into the distant future, while your Big Money account provides you with an opportunity to radically change the way you live in the very near future. Think about the contents of your bedroom closet. If your lockbox represented a cross section of your most conservative work-appropriate attire, your Big Money account would represent that one favorite shirt, jacket, or pair of shoes that you have absolute, unwavering confidence wearing when you need to look and feel your best.

For the remainder of this book, we will focus solely on your Big

Money investing account, which under no condition should ever share or compete for funds with your lockbox. Regardless of your financial worth, successfully learning how to compartmentalize your lockbox and OPM funds will make it possible for you to approach Big Money investing with a risk-tolerant mind-set no different from J. P. Morgan's when he built his financial empire.

5

SEE IT, BELIEVE IT!

How to View Your World Through Investor's Glasses

"It is not what you look at that matters, it's what you see."
—HENRY DAVID THOREAU

They call us early birds. You know us. We're the odd people who arrive at your tag sale before sunrise, peering through your windows and begging for a chance to preview your sale merchandise. Flip through any newspaper's weekend classifieds section and, under the category of estate or tag sales (or garage sales or yard sales), you will find dozens of sale ads either beginning or ending with "No Early Birds!"

The ragtag group of characters who are the early birds of society generally fall into one of three categories:

1. Professionals who are looking to pick up bargain antiques and collectibles to sell at their booths at the antiques mall.
2. Treasure hunters who are on an endless conquest to find that lost Picasso or perhaps that Rolex watch that accidentally got thrown into the junk jewelry bin (it happens!).

3. Scavengers who furnish their homes and clothe their families exclusively with tag sale merchandise.

In high school I was a typical early bird, buying anything of value I knew I could flip for a profit. What I purchased I sold to professional antiques dealers, consignment stores, or even other early birds at the sale. (eBay did not yet exist.) The hours were brutal and the money less than spectacular, but since I was a teenager with few expenses or responsibilities, that didn't matter. Flipping tangible tag sale merchandise for a profit was a lot more gratifying than my early trial attempts at making money in the stock market.

Ironically, the early-bird skills I picked up by shopping at tag sales are what would finally enable me to crack the code of investing. Early-birding is an intense sport, and the similarities with stock investing are closer than you might imagine. The early bird game all comes down to information and timing—identifying worth in what others unknowingly discard or dismiss as having little or no value. If you are an early bird, you have a small window of time at the beginning of each sale to spot mispriced items of value before the oncoming herd of competition arrives. Hence, the obsession of the early bird to be first in line at every sale. Spend too much time appraising a reproduction of a silver-plated chalice and you might miss a priceless Kämmerand Reinhardt doll hidden among the children's toys—soon to be discovered by another early bird. If you do your job well, you leave little of substance for others to pick over.

When I was at my best, I could shop a five-bedroom estate sale in under sixty seconds without leaving a single mispriced item of value behind. To my credit, I spent many summer afternoons loitering in the aisles of my local bookstore memorizing price guides on antiques and collectibles. I had perfected the ability to separate items of value from the rubbish very quickly. But what truly separated me from other early birds was my ability to swiftly break down a sale and uncover mispriced treasures. Other early birds may have dismissed my success as luck, but my finely honed ability to scout winning sales and assess mispriced merchandise was due to my unique understanding of how estate and tag sale merchandise is priced.

Be it a stay-at-home mom or a hired professional estate sale agent, the vast majority of people who price the items sold at estate and tag sales are women. And women, while exceptionally skilled at assigning value to female-oriented items (such as jewelry, antique furnishings, silverware, and couture clothing), are prone to occasionally underpricing items that fall toward the masculine end of the gender spectrum—a Ted Williams baseball card, a vintage Zephyr guitar, or a collectible Lionel train set, for example. I knew that exclusively focusing my energy on these overlooked categories of items would give me the greatest opportunity to hit paydirt on a given sale day. This was a crucial differentiator, because early birds, who spend hours agonizing over sale descriptions in the weekend newspaper classifieds as part of our presale preparation, might get only one or two at bats every week to secure the coveted first-in-line position at a sale. Choose the wrong sale while you wait out the pre-daylight hours, and you might as well have skipped the 5:00 AM early bird stakeout ritual and slept until noon.

For this reason, the evening prior to the prospective sale's opening day, I would preview, in person, the houses of sales I deemed to be promising. During my visit, I would attempt to speak with the homeowner or, if that was not possible, peer through the home's front windows (not intrusively, but from the front walkway or porch) to ascertain the existence and exact location of sale items in product cat-egories I determined to have a high likelihood of being mispriced—sports equipment, comic books, electronics. Every first-in-line posi-tion I secured—every directional step I took on sale day upon entering a home, garage, or roped-off yard—was by design. Nothing was left to chance. And because of that, I rarely left a sale empty-handed.

> Seeking a way to generate funds for your OPM account? Be-come an early bird. Thanks to eBay, selling treasures you acquire as an early bird will be light years easier than it was for me.

The mornings spent shopping tag sales taught me how to profit from situations where I possessed a unique information advantage over others, many of whom were often seasoned professionals three or four times my age. This mind-set would serve as the foundation for all of my future success as a stock picker.

Here's where my early bird experiences met my fascination with the stock market for the first time. On sale mornings, I would always stop at the local 7-Eleven to grab a copy of that morning's classifieds, along with a bottle of my favorite pick-me-up, Snapple Lemon Ice Tea. It was a regular part of my structured morning routine before hitting sales—at least until one early summer morning when I dis-covered that the 7-Eleven no longer stocked my favorite flavor. Over-night, the store's shelf space for Snapple products had dwindled from two full refrigerators to less than one half. I hadn't even hit my first sale of the morning, but my early-bird mind-set enabled me to un-cover an investment opportunity. As I looked at the bottles of fla-vored drinks behind those glass-door refrigerators, I recalled my father telling me, "The very best time to buy a company's stock is when you think you know something about that company that others don't."

For years I had unknowingly applied my dad's advice to acquire mispriced tag sale merchandise as an early bird. But I never imagined that I would be in a position to uncover something about a public company that wasn't already obvious to investors and Wall Street professionals.

In the late 1980s, the Snapple brand of fruit drinks grew into a cultural phenomenon. Having the world's largest convenience store chain cut Snapple's shelf space by 75 percent couldn't be a positive development for the brand. After years of unsuccessful attempts to chase down the next great stock investment, was it possible I had just had such an opportunity fall in my lap?

I immediately contacted my older brother, a securities broker, who taught me how to use stock options to make a short-term wager against Snapple's stock price. If the price of Snapple's stock dropped, the value of my investment would go up. (You will learn about these types of leveraged investments later.)

The very next week, Snapple announced that their inventory of unsold product had risen dramatically—negatively impacting the company's profits. Convenience store retailers, including 7-Eleven, were being deluged with flavored drinks backed by larger beverage companies, which was pushing Snapple off the shelves and back into its distributor's warehouses.

The result? I tripled my $300 investment in just a few days simply by acting on information I had stumbled across—information that Wall Street had never found or had overlooked. And in doing so, I proved that in the world of investing, just as in the world of tag sales, it is the early bird who catches the worm.

CHANCE FAVORS THE PREPARED MIND
Learning to Make Your Own Luck

Scientific history is littered with "eureka moments," where unanticipated flashes of inspiration seemingly arise from fate, accidents, or chance:

- While watching an apple fall from a tree, esteemed physicist Isaac Newton discovered the "law of gravity."
- Penicillin was discovered by chance in 1928 after Scottish biologist Alexander Fleming accidentally left a dish of staphylococcus bacteria uncovered for a few days. He returned to find the dish dotted with bacterial growth, except in one area, where a patch of mold was growing. The mold produced a substance that inhibited harmful bacterial growth; Fleming named it penicillin.
- Silly Putty was created by accident during research into potential rubber substitutes for use by the United States in World War II.
- Spencer Silver, a research chemist, was working toward the invention of a new super-strong glue compound for his company, 3M. A by-product of his trials resulted in producing the opposite: a seemingly useless and temporary reusable glue that released with a yank without causing damage, and left no residue. His colleague, Art Fry, decided to use the failed compound to keep his hymnal bookmarks from falling out while singing in the church choir. The modern-day Post-it note was born.

Serendipity, the gift of making useful discoveries by accident, is the modern-day term most often used to define the circumstances surrounding such "chance" scientific discoveries and those fortunate enough to have made them. But what may appear to have been an accidental discovery is most often the result of a methodical process instilled within the scientific mind-set. In the book *Scientific Social Surveys and Research,* sociology scholar Pauline V. Young suggests that "Scientists cultivate serendipity by being constantly alert for chance occurrences that may lead to new explanations or discoveries."[11] The "chance" observation leading to the unexpected result would be rendered useless if not for the scientific method that prepares the mind of the scientist to detect the importance of information revealed accidentally. The French scientist Louis Pasteur famously said, "In the fields of observation, chance favors only the prepared mind."

This difference between passively viewing and actively being able to detect game-changing shifts in information has empowered ordinary scientists to become Nobel Prize winners. It is the ability to spot game-changing information that has the potential to determine your fate in achieving financial prosperity as an investor. The cornerstone of my success—every winning investment I have made beginning with Snapple—can be attributed to my ability to tap into innate observation skills and uncover investment opportunities amid the mundane happenings of my everyday life.

GARBAGE IN, GARBAGE OUT
Incomplete Information Nearly Always Leads to Imperfect Decision Making

When placing a value on companies and making investment decisions, investment professionals crunch numbers, study charts, and analyze corporate financials, incorporating all the information available. But unknowingly overlooking just one piece of game-changing information has the potential to render their analysis completely worthless.

Suppose you are shopping for a beach vacation home and you make what you believe to be a below-market offer on a property, based on an appraisal provided by a seasoned real estate professional who employed all of the time-tested tools of real estate appraisal (e.g., neighborhood comparisons, tax-assessed value, prior sale price, recent market trends).

You are ecstatic to find out that your offer was accepted, only to learn later that your new next-door neighbor, who is rumored to be involved with organized crime, parks a dilapidated thirty-foot boat in front of his house nine months out of the year, obstructing the otherwise peaceful palm-tree-lined view that was your primary motivation for buying the property in the first pace. A short conversation with a nearby neighbor would more than likely have revealed this game-changing information and helped you avoid making a costly life mistake.

This past year my parents purchased a convertible using profits from their Big Money investing account. While negotiating with the dealer for their car, they cross-referenced vehicle valuations from every available car pricing guide to determine a fair market purchase price. Unfortunately, none of the pricing guides took into account that the particular model and body style they were negotiating to buy was set to be discontinued by the manufacturer—which was sure to have an adverse affect on the car's current value and rate of depreciation.

When trying to accurately assess the value of an asset that has a fluctuating market price—be it a house, car, or stock of a publicly traded company—the chosen method of valuation is far less important than the quality and completeness of the information being plugged into the valuation model. The hypothetical real estate appraisal

I cited was deeply flawed as a result of the reluctance of real estate agents to interview neighbors in pursuit of game-changing information, even when such knowledge has the potential to significantly impact a home's value.

When providing vehicle valuations, car pricing guides don't take into account pending model replacements or vehicle discontinuations, even though such critical forward-looking information can easily be obtained by flipping through car enthusiast magazines such as *Car and Driver* or *Road & Track*. In both of these scenarios, the industry's "professional" authorities or resources provided a flawed recommendation of value as a result of their unwillingness to explore or consider information and knowledge collected through unconventional means.

Likewise, those who act in a professional capacity on Wall Street tend to adopt, to their own detriment, streamlined valuation methodologies that (1) leverage their specific training and skill set, and (2) are easily instated, replicated, and evaluated across their organization and industry at large. This phenomenon is more prevalent in the field of investment management than perhaps in any other industry, as investment professionals nearly always conduct their analysis using narrowly defined financial and statistical models that are exclusively reliant on information acquired through established channels. They place little to no emphasis on "off-the-radar" unpublished information not yet widely accepted as fact by other professionals or the investing public.

Just as Coldwell Banker does not implement "Neighbor Interview Training" for its real estate brokers, it is hard to imagine Goldman Sachs or JPMorgan ever training or encouraging their investment staff to seek out the next big consumer trend by surfing Facebook posts, watching TMZ, or making observations of ordinary people at the amusement park. Doing so would give credence to an investment methodology not specifically reliant on the professionals' credentialed financial expertise—the equivalent of professional suicide.

Think about it. Why would you pay a professional to do something you are equally if not more qualified to do on your own? If such a simple-minded investment methodology—one *not* centered on the complex analysis of information, but on the advance discovery of information—did exist, you can be sure the financial industry would do everything in its power to discredit it.

In my years working to build the world's largest research panel of eight million consumers at my former employer, the market research company e-Rewards, we often referenced the phrase "garbage in, garbage out" to bring shame on our industry competitors. To the detriment of project quality, our competition often refused to institute what we considered to be an imperative but costly measure to identify and prevent "professional survey takers" from participating in client projects.

As a hypothetical example, if Nike were to field a survey to gauge the running shoe preferences of frequent runners, such a survey would hold little validity if half of the so-called frequent runners participating were actually couch potatoes misrepresenting themselves as runners in order to fraudulently collect the cash honorarium paid by Nike for completing the survey. Just as a person can't brew a great cup of coffee using inferior or stale beans, a company can't conduct good market research based on faulty or deficient survey data.

Investment analysis is no different. While those on Wall Street may have unprecedented access to money and resources to decrypt trends for financial gain, the archaic means by which they go about information discovery—combined with their bias due to the financial industry's being disproportionately represented by affluent, middle-aged male "financial professionals"—puts them at a distinct disadvantage to us ordinary folks, who have our feet firmly planted in the real world.

For example, one of my Wall Street friends once suggested I buy the stock of a high-flying video game company by the name of Electronic Arts. I asked him if he had spoken to any of the teenagers who played the company's games. He hadn't, nor did he seem to understand why it would be important for him to do so. He claimed to have mountains of up-to-date data and industry analysis collected by his firm's research division. If he had conducted some personal inquiries, however, he would have discovered that the very gamers whose brand loyalty helped propel the company in years prior to become the world's largest developer of video games had recently begun to lose interest in many of the company's most successful game franchises.

The Electronic Arts brand, once synonymous with gaming industry innovation, was beginning to lose its edge and appeal among its core base of active gamers at the very same time it was posting record revenues and profits on Wall Street. In the months following my friend's tip, the company's product line started to show signs of weakness, and just one year later, with some help from a down stock market, stock in the company had fallen by more than 70 percent.

INFORMATION ARBITRAGE
The Investor with an Information Edge Always Wins

"In ancient times, skilled warriors made themselves invincible, and then watched for vulnerability in their opponent."
—SUN TZU, *The Art of War*

As in war, investing is a zero-sum game, with a winner and loser emerging from every stock trade. Yet, to the financial institutions, professional traders, and hedge funds that show up to do battle each day for dominance on Wall Street, the self-directed investor barely registers as a sideline observer. We are invisible to them, meaning we are free to pick apart and exploit their vulnerabilities at will, without risk of their making adjustments or attempting to replicate our game plan for their benefit.

Did my friend on Wall Street learn his lesson after the Electronic Arts debacle? The next time he makes an investment recommendation for a company serving the youth market, will he first take the time to engage with the company's teen customers? I wouldn't bet on it. Doing so is simply not in his professional makeup, and it is below his self-perceived "pay grade." If his Wall Street peers or institutional clients caught wind of him applying such unconventional investment methodology in his stock analysis, it would open him up to being ridiculed as a rogue—an unhinged analyst who deviates from what his peers consider to be time-tested standards of financial practice. In the rigid financial industry, where maintaining the status quo ensures billion-dollar profits and million-dollar bonuses for all, anyone exposed as being disruptive or radical remains so at the potential cost of his career. The rewards of being right are all too often not worth the risks.

No amount of fundamental or technical investment analysis will counterbalance flawed investment research cited by an investment professional who turns a blind eye to potentially game-changing information. As a self-directed investor, successfully uncovering just one overlooked nugget of game-changing information is the equivalent of getting to see the dealer's down card during a game of blackjack at a casino. Your ability to leverage the stock market to capitalize on the information you uncover is limited only by the amount of monetary gunpowder you have amassed in your Big Money account.

By now, it should be clear that Wall Street's vulnerability, its

Achilles' heel to be exploited, is its utter inability to quickly uncover emerging game-changing information—information with the potential to materially impact sales and profits. This is primarily due to the industry's inherent biases, absence of creative vision, and lack of resourcefulness, not to mention its lack of motive. Remember that, in spite of its ineptitude, Wall Street is among the most financially lucrative industries in the world for those who work within its walls.

In my years shopping tag sales as an early bird, I would have likened those on Wall Street to the late-arriving, often arrogant antique store owners, who were always happy to pay a healthy premium to acquire the great finds I had snatched up minutes or hours prior. These store owners would ultimately sell those items at even higher prices to their unsuspecting retail clients.

Uncovering your opponent's vulnerability is half the game. The other half is knowing how to exploit it for your benefit. Since the Dutch East India Company first started trading as a public company over four centuries ago, investors seeking stock market prosperity have been chasing the "correct" answers to two of Wall Street's most frequently asked investment questions:

1. How will I know when to initiate an investment (buy)?
2. How will I know when to exit an investment (sell)?

As a self-directed investor who has amassed (and since discarded) two decades of investment books and "how-to-invest" articles, I have witnessed firsthand the parade of conflicting, often dizzying if not tortuous theories on how to buy and sell stocks. These books and articles were written by well-intentioned so-called "stock market experts" promoting investing systems that were needlessly too complex.

Suspiciously, not one of them has published or offered access to their own audited multi-year investment returns as proof of their claims of being able to substantially outperform either the stock market at large or the performance of a randomly assembled stock portfolio. Few people would place much weight on relationship advice from those who have never been able to maintain a successful relationship themselves, or diet advice from a friend who has been overweight her entire life. Yet we are so often willing to place our future financial wellbeing in the hands of people and institutions whose only proven success is their ability to persuade people to pay them for providing virtually nothing of substantive value in return.

Still, those on and off Wall Street continue their desperate search for the mythical stock market prodigy or trading system that will lead them and their clients to an endless supply of easy money. For years, stories circulated among Wall Street insiders of an elusive investing guru who'd cracked the code of the market, producing spectacular returns year after year by using a highly secretive algorithmic-based trading system. There were just two problems: his highly guarded services were made available only to personal friends, celebrities, and the most privileged, ultra-high-net-worth clients of the Wall Street elite; and more important, after twenty years and roughly $50 billion, his highly regarded trading system was exposed as nothing more than a Ponzi scheme.

His name is Bernie Madoff, and the good news is that you probably weren't important enough or rich enough to have directly fallen victim to his fraudulent scheme. Not so lucky were high-profile Madoff clients, including Kevin Bacon, Kyra Sedgwick, John Malkovich, baseball legend Sandy Koufax, DreamWorks CEO Jeffrey Katzenberg, screen legend Zsa Zsa Gabor, director Steven Spielberg, New York Mets owners Fred Wilpon and Saul Katz, and the International Olympic Committee, along with countless charitable foundations, real estate and publishing magnates, Nobel Prize winners, senators, and hedge funds, who lost from millions to billions of dollars each.

The victim list even includes the likes of banking giants JPMorgan Chase, Bank of America, Citibank, HSBC, and the Santander bank group of Spain, who alone watched over $3 billion of their money disappear overnight. How a bank that mandates that I produce two years of income verification for a $10,000 credit line increase falls victim to a multibillion-dollar pyramid scheme I will never understand.

If we've learned one thing from the infamous "investment guru" and former honored chairman of the NASDAQ turned imprisoned con artist Bernie Madoff, it is to approach the words of every self-proclaimed investment authority with a healthy dose of skepticism. Whenever I meet people dishing out investment advice, I always ask them to disclose their personal investment returns for the prior three-year period. If I ran a financial and investing television network, I would institute a "Why Should I Listen to You?" meter, which would prominently display onscreen the three-year investment returns of every guest pundit during the full length of their on-air interview. The network would admittedly have a hard time attracting guests, but those who did appear on its programs would certainly be worth listening to.

Sometimes simple questions are best served by simple answers. My take on buying and selling stocks—the method I used to turn $20,000 into more than $2,000,000 over a three-and-a-half-year period from 2007 to 2010, during one of the worst recessions in decades—can be summed up in the answers to the two previous questions:

Question: How will I know when to initiate an investment (buy)?

Answer: Upon discovery of game-changing information not yet known by Wall Street.

Question: How will I know when to exit an investment (sell)?

Answer: When the game-changing information becomes widely accepted as fact on Wall Street.

The path to achieving stock market prosperity is that simple. It is not contingent upon your analysis of financial ratios, growth rates, price charts, or competitive positioning. Nor does it require you to hold a scholarly degree in finance or possess expert-level proficiency in investing, or even basic math. Just as I was able to leverage found information to capitalize on mispriced tag sale merchandise as a teenage early bird, your physical and emotional proximity to the pulse of the products and companies in your own backyard is what qualifies and positions you as a front-line observer able to uncover the all-important game-changing information that precedes great stock market investments.

The heart of this book's investment methodology lies in the assumed existence of information imbalances across two distinct information markets: Wall Street and Main Street. The previously cited story about a popular video game maker is an example of an information imbalance where we have the business itself telling a story of growth and success while the blogs and chat rooms of congregating gamers convey a very different story—one of a stagnant company product line. The information imbalance phenomenon is defined by the window of time between the earliest emergence of information on Main Street and the point at which that information reaches in-formation parity on Wall Street.

> Information arbitrage: the science of initiating investments upon discovery of an information imbalance, and exiting in-vestments at the point of information parity.

I call the science of initiating investments upon discovery of an information imbalance, and exiting investments at the point of in-formation parity, "information arbitrage." As an early bird shopping tag sales, I focused my information arbitrage efforts on male-oriented products, which were often mispriced by the women managing the sales. But on Wall Street, the high concentration of middle-aged men who influence investment decisions creates opportunities to profit from information imbalances that are most pronounced with re-spect to female- and youth-oriented products, companies, and trends. A small tweak and reapplication of my tag sale strategy was all it took for me to transition the skills I'd accrued as an early bird to become one of the world's most successful self-directed investors.

INVESTOR'S GLASSES

In order to exploit information arbitrage for financial gain, you must first learn to heighten your senses, to recognize anything and every-thing you come across during the course of your day that has the poten-tial to materially impact a company's sales or profits: i.e., game-changing information. Learning this skill can be both extraordinarily easy and very difficult. Just think: how many people, both on and off Wall Street, had the opportunity to spot Snapple's rapidly depleting shelf space while walking down the aisle of their corner convenience store? Millions? Tens of millions? My early bird mind-set tricked my brain into noticing an irregularity that day that others before and after me did not.

Much in the same way that a scientist or crime scene investigator observes and scrutinizes information and data to extrapolate all of its hidden potential, I have since honed my ability to see the extraordinary investment potential in what others inadvertently pass over or view as ordinary. I refer to this phenomenon as viewing the world through investor's glasses, and it has nothing to do with finance and everything to do with the way we observe and perceive the information we stumble across in our natural environment.

Think of all the barely visible details parents notice while watching their infant child—things that a nonparent would never detect. In the 1892 short story "A Scandal in Bohemia," private investigator extraordinaire Sherlock Holmes says to Dr. Watson, "You see but you do not observe." This is a reminder that we can always improve our observation skills. For private investigators, as with scientists and parents, the stakes are exceptionally high, so they must employ their senses for the purpose of critical observation.

Critical observation is the all-important element of a rigid process known as the scientific method. This concept, employed by all scientists, is simple: an observation is made, a hypothesis is proposed, experiments are done, and conclusions are reached. As a self-directed investor, successfully applying the scientific method of information arbitrage requires that I employ these same four principles.

70

OBSERVATION

October 27, 2008: 11:07 PM

"Actually, this is a J.Crew ensemble," said soon-to-be First Lady, Michelle Obama, while wearing a yellow J.Crew sweater, skirt, and blouse. She was responding to a question posed by *Tonight Show* host Jay Leno on the topic of vice-presidential hopeful Sarah Palin's $150,000 GOP-issued Neiman Marcus wardrobe. "You can get some good stuff online," Mrs. Obama added.

January 20, 2009: 11:56 AM

First Lady Michelle Obama is wearing a pair of J.Crew sage green leather gloves to hold the Bible for her husband while he stands before a worldwide audience of 140 million plus (via television and Internet) to be sworn in as America's first ever African American president. Also present were the Obama daughters, wearing pale pink and royal blue wool coats from J.Crew.

During this defining moment in American history, the First Lady chose to forego designer threads and, instead, show her love for a mass consumer retailer in what can only be described as the ultimate brand endorsement during one of the most observed events ever by a global audience. And later, President Obama attended his inaugural ball marathon wearing a J.Crew bow tie. The price of J.Crew stock on the day of the inauguration was $9.03.

Viewers seeking to mirror the Obama family's sense of fashion flocked to J.Crew's Web site in droves. By the afternoon of the inauguration, the J.Crew Web page featuring women's gloves had crashed. By the next morning, the entire women's section of the Web site had crashed. Later that day, the surge in Web traffic caused the entire site to go down.

May 28 2009: 8:45 AM

While flipping through Sirius satellite news channels on my morning commute, I caught a story on J.Crew, whose stock that morning had jumped a staggering 25 percent after the company announced a positive surprise in quarterly sales to Wall Street the night prior. What I heard next nearly caused me to steer my car off the road. The unexpected rise in sales was in part being attributed to the massive amount of free publicity the company had received as a result of having their brand associated with Michelle Obama, a newly anointed global style icon.

In the months following the presidential inauguration, the First Lady and her children became walking manikins for J.Crew merchandise, and each time any of them appeared in the media spotlight wearing a J.Crew garment, that garment would immediately sell out on the company's Web site. Throughout this time, photographs of Michelle Obama and daughters Malia and Sasha sporting J.Crew outfits regularly graced the covers and pages of mainstream and tabloid publications alike, exposing the brand and its flourishing new image to tens of millions of prospective customers. Among those new customers were droves of African Americans, a demographic often ignored by mass-market apparel companies due to the companies' difficulty connecting with that group through mainstream marketing channels.

It is not often that a mature company such as J.Crew is handed the opportunity to acquire a new multibillion-dollar market segment. But Michelle Obama's halo effect on J.Crew was a game changer. In the four-month period between the First Lady's appearance at the presidential inauguration and the company's surprise positive earnings announcement, J.Crew stock climbed a staggering 186 percent, from $9.03 to $25.86.

Upon hearing this news, I immediately placed a not-so-friendly call to my wife. "How could you not have brought this Michele Obama/J.Crew story to my attention?" I asked her. "You, of all people, read fashion magazines daily!" In reality, I had no one to blame but myself. Upon arriving home that night, I flipped through half a dozen of our coffee table magazines and found two photos of Michelle Obama and her daughters draped in J.Crew clothing—right smack in the middle of my very own "guilty pleasure" weekly tabloids. The magazines had even highlighted the J.Crew connection.

Adding fuel to the fire, later that evening my wife helped me recall that we had both watched the First Lady's appearance on the *Tonight Show* months earlier. Like most of Wall Street, I had simply dropped the ball on an opportunity to critically observe and capitalize on game-changing information that had been sitting in front of me for months.

Even though J.Crew's stock would go on to climb another twenty points over the next six months, the ground-floor opportunity to seize on an information imbalance in the stock had passed. Wall Street had begun to show clear signs that the Michelle Obama/J.Crew story was approaching a point of information parity. Some of the headlines from the financial press that morning included "J.Crew Rides Obama Coattails to Higher Sales," "J.Crew Proves Analysts Wrong," and "J. Crew Surges on Upgrades."

Nearly a full year later, the missed investment opportunity had faded to become a distant memory. That was until, while watching an episode of *Oprah* as part of my due diligence process for another investment, I heard Oprah shout out, "The very first time I saw the First Lady, even before she became the First Lady, wearing J.Crew, I went and bought some J.Crew stock, and it was a very good decision."

J.Crew stock had by then climbed more than fivefold, to nearly $50 a share.

In the scientific method of information arbitrage, the first step is making an observation. Scientific observation is defined as any sensory experience, most often sight, that causes the scientist to think and ask a question. For the purposes of investing, the question you ask yourself will look very much the same each and every time. If you find yourself asking, "Could what I'm seeing have the potential to materially impact some company's sales or profits?"—congratulations! You have just made an investing observation.

How is it that Oprah was able so quickly to spot an investment opportunity from information largely ignored by so many others on and off Wall Street? Oprah's keen sense of observation should not really surprise anyone. She might not have the mind-set of a scientist or private investigator, but she does have the disposition of an entrepreneur, and all successful entrepreneurs share an instinctual trait for uncovering opportunities in what most people perceive as commonplace. This is the most important prerequisite of investment discovery.

Let's say you and a friend are listening to music poolside when you hear Katy Perry's newly launched song "Waking Up in Vegas" for the first time. You reminisce about how much you miss those spontaneous weekend trips to Vegas. A month later, you and your friends are celebrating a weekend away at your favorite casino hotel in the desert. Question: Could Katy Perry's song stimulate Vegas travel bookings enough to have a material impact on room sales and revenue at Vegas Casino Hotels?

You are at a club dancing the night away. The DJ is spinning a new Jay-Z song whose lyrics glorify the Cristal brand of champagne. You then notice numerous open bottles of Cristal among the VIP tables at the club. Question: Could the positive buzz that Jay-Z and other hip-hop stars create around products such as Cristal champagne stimulate a spike in demand for those products at the benefit of the companies who manufacture them?

You and your significant other go out to the movies to see the Santa Barbara wine country–inspired hit film *Sideways*. You leave the movie craving a glass of California Pinot Noir, which you go on to order at a neighborhood bar next door to the theater. You notice several other couples who also saw the movie doing the same. The bartender even cracks a joke about having practically run out of Pinot Noir in the two weeks since the movie started playing. Could this film's staggering global popularity, combined with the positive emotional response it generates toward wine, change drinking habits to the point of having a material positive impact on wine company sales?

Then you see the movie *Avatar* in 3D at an IMAX theater, the first IMAX theater you've visited in years. You walk out of the film feeling that you have just witnessed the future of filmed entertainment. Could the movie *Avatar* mark a tipping point in filmed entertainment where visually stunning 3D movies become mainstream, causing a material surge in ticket sales at IMAX theaters?

You haven't rented a movie at Blockbuster since a friend convinced you to open an account with a newly launched DVD rental-by-mail company named Netflix. On the occasion that you do have a need to make a same-day movie rental, you generally order a pay-per-view movie from your cable provider. Could the combination of Netflix and on-demand programming cause a paradigm shift in terms of how people rent movies at home? And, if so, could that have a negative impact on video rental sales at Blockbuster?

The Atkins-inspired low-carb diet craze, observed by only your most health-obsessed friends a year ago, has now gotten your mother, brother, and boss all eating steak and eggs for breakfast and ordering bacon-topped burgers (minus the bun) for lunch. Could this latest diet fad increase global demand for beef while decreasing global demand for bread products? If so, will this trend adversely affect the sales of companies that produce bread and bakery food products?

So You Think You Can Dance is the highest rated television show of the summer, and *Dancing with the Stars* is one of the highest rated television shows of the fall season. Even with the addition of two new dance studios in your neighborhood, you are having trouble finding an open spot to enroll your daughter in dance class. Could America's renewed interest in dance cause an increase in sales at companies that make leotards, ballet shoes, and dance-oriented apparel?

A recurring hot topic among the expectant mothers in the group you belong to is whether to pony up the $1,500 fee to cryopreserve their newborns' cord blood, a procedure that was nearly unheard of just a year earlier, when your sister gave birth to her child. The science, while promising, has yet to prove its ability to deliver substantial future health benefits. Yet you, along with a surprising number of the group's members, are choosing to spend the money, thinking it is "better to be safe than sorry." Could this trend toward cryopreserving cord blood have a positive impact on sales for the handful of medical companies involved in this emerging science?

Just months after enrolling in a clinical drug trial, a coworker's uncle, who was diagnosed with prostate cancer a year ago, is showing significant signs of improvement. Could the improvement in this patient's medical condition preface the future approval of a new cancer drug, with the potential to increase revenue for its pharmaceutical parent company?

You want to buy a special birthday present for your teenage niece, who has had a difficult year fitting in at school. You find out from her mother that Ugg boots and True Religion jeans are all the rage among her classmates this season. According to her daughter, "Everyone is getting them." Could the sudden popularity of these two premium niche brands among teenagers cause a huge increase in sales at their respective companies?

While visiting friends in Ohio, you spend the day at a local amusement park, where you notice an entire family outfitted in brightly colored, somewhat odd-looking rubber sandals. This scene repeats itself throughout the day. While waiting in line for a ride, you overhear one of the rubber-shoe-wearing soccer moms gloat to a curious onlooker about the shoes' comfort. She comments that she and her children have become addicted to wearing the funny-looking shoes— which are called Crocs. Hearing this makes you realize how much your feet hurt. Could a viral movement toward functional comfort over style in casual footwear, set off by suburban soccer moms and families in Middle America, fuel a material boost in sales of Crocs?

Your Thanksgiving holiday is hijacked by the video game Guitar Hero. All hours of the day and night, nearly every member of your family takes turns simulating their favorite rock hits on the game's plastic push-button guitar. Equally obsessed with the game are your six-year-old niece and sixty-year-old uncle. Could the mass-market appeal of the video game Guitar Hero become a full-blown cultural phenomenon across all demographics, causing revenue at its parent company, Activision, to skyrocket?

While visiting a Wendy's for the first time in years to try out their newly launched salad entree offering, you become instantly hooked. Could the fast-food retailer's ability to convert health-conscious diners such as you into new repeat customers boost revenue?

In the weeks after the terrorist attacks of September 11, 2001, security at airports became more stringent than you had witnessed in your lifetime. Prior to the attacks, you were annoyed by the trial program being facilitated by airport security that forced you to carry your check-in luggage to a separate area of the terminal for X-ray screening. Now you accept the inconvenience as part of what you expect to become the "new normal" in airport security. Could the government's new emphasis on airport security in a post-9/11 world lead to a national rollout of the trial X-ray program for check-in baggage—resulting in a corresponding windfall of revenue for the bomb detection company that manufactures the program's high-tech equipment?

As part of a company-wide cost-cutting plan, your employer transitions its legacy customer relationship management software to a more cost-efficient, Web-based platform by the name of Salesforce .com. Several months later a friend of yours who works at a Fortune 500 company asks you for advice while trying to train himself on Salesforce.com after his company decided to switch CRM platforms. Could industry-wide adoption of Web-based CRM software trigger a tidal wave of new accounts for Salesforce.com while bringing about account defections and revenue loss for legacy desktop-based CRM software firms such as Oracle, SAP, and Siebel?

Each observation you make as a self-directed investor is an "at bat." Each is a unique opportunity to discover an information imbalance that could lead to investing riches. Not all of the real-life observations just cited qualify as genuine information arbitrage investing opportunities. In the chapter ahead, we will explore many of these observations while piecing together the necessary elements comprising a winning information arbitrage investing opportunity.

Achieving financial prosperity can be accomplished by uncovering as few as three or four winning investments over a multi-year period, but finding those winning investments will require making many dozens, if not hundreds, of observations.

Learning to use your newfound investor's glasses requires a change in the way you perceive the world around you—and the patience to wait on pins and needles for as long as it takes to put yourself in a position to capitalize on an information imbalance when it crosses your path.

The big-wave surfer is accustomed to months of downtime, eyeing global weather and buoy reports while waiting for the next big swell to hit. Just as the big-wave surfer is at the mercy of nature and has to be prepared to travel to the ends of the world at a moment's notice to seize the next big-wave opportunity, you must be ready and accepting of the timing and location of investment opportunities, and the manner in which they reveal themselves to you. Your future success will hinge on the degree to which you are able to heighten your innate sense of observation—and that can be achieved only through practice, practice, and more practice.

Simply being aware of the potential payoff will prime the pump of your unconscious brain to begin naturally noticing opportunities. But unless you consciously push yourself to actively observe the potential investments hidden within every passing moment of your day, you are sure to miss many more observations than you uncover. I make multiple investment observations each week, yet I overlooked the Michelle Obama/J.Crew opportunity that was right in front of my face—a seemingly obvious connection for Oprah, who, I suspect, doesn't spend as much time thinking about the science of information arbitrage investing as I do.

Among other things, I now read every page of the weekly tabloids with a renewed sense of purpose. I won't miss another Michelle

Obama/J.Crew moment! Missed opportunities do not discourage me as much as inspire me to step up my sense of observation and perception of life as it unfolds around me.

You are bound to miss out on investment opportunities occasionally, perhaps even some right in your own backyard. However, rest assured that just as experiencing surfing bliss for the big wave surfer is reliant on his landing a single, perfect wave, it takes only one intuitive observation turned into a winning investment to radically change your economic well-being.

6

ZERO FINANCIAL LITERACY REQUIRED

Investigative Due Diligence for the Math and Finance Impaired

Some people enjoy going to shopping malls during the holiday season. I am not one of those people. The traffic, crowds, and long lines are a holiday ritual I can live without. Of course, there are times during November and December when even I am left with no choice but to brave a visit to the local mall.

Such was the case a few years back when I went shopping for a watch for my wife, Amy. Over the course of an exhausting weekend, I must have visited every chain and boutique jewelry retailer in the city. Luckily for me, the down economy made for a relatively crowd-free shopping experience. There I was, just weeks before Christmas, at one of the largest malls in Texas—and there was hardly a store in sight with a line at the cash register.

It was that eerie lack of holiday crowds that made what I was about to see even more surprising. Amid a sea of empty stores stood a bustling Coach store with a checkout line thirty people deep and snaking out the front door. The sight invoked feelings of both excitement and disbelief. It was the information arbitrage investor's equivalent of spotting a mirage of freshwater in the desert—one that turned out to be real!

Were the long lines at the checkout counter of my local Coach store indicative of strong holiday sales at that retailer? With that question, an investment observation was born. There was clearly a story behind the unusually busy Coach store I stumbled across that day, but it would require me to dig deep and get dirty with follow-up due diligence research. I had to determine if the observation I had stumbled across would make for a wise information arbitrage investment.

Due diligence, the exhaustive process of conducting comprehensive financial research on a company or investing idea, is an essential and often laborious prerequisite to making an investing decision. Fortunately, the process for conducting due diligence on the investment observations we make is more akin to investigating a crime scene than performing a financial audit. For me, it's often the most enjoyable part of the investing game.

CONSTRUCTING YOUR INVESTMENT HYPOTHESES

What could be drawing so many shoppers to make purchases at the Coach store in the midst of an economic recession? Lines out the door at this established retailer couldn't be the norm, could they? Coach was no longer a hot new brand—it had been mass-marketing its distinctive line of designer accessories to women for decades. Were Coach stores in other areas of the country experiencing the same unexplainable influx of holiday customers? If so, could the phenomenon be attributed to a great seasonal product line, or was it just deep discounting? Could what I was seeing be the result of that recessionary "trading-down" effect I kept hearing about on the news? (When economic hardship causes the Louis Vuitton and Gucci shoppers of the world to become more frugal with their shopping, stores such as Coach and Dooney & Bourke benefit.)

When an observation leads to one or more unanswered, unresolved questions, scientists propose hypotheses—possible explanations for the observation. Through experimentation and evaluation, each hypothesis is proven to be either correct or incorrect. As an investor seeking answers to observations you make, you are able to use this same process. Following my observation at the Coach store, five investment hypotheses were born:

1. The long lines at the checkout counter of my local Coach store are representative of checkout lines at other Coach stores throughout the country—the result of a superior seasonal product line, which will materially impact holiday sales at the retailer.

2. The long lines at the checkout counter of my local Coach store are representative of checkout lines at other Coach stores throughout the country—the result of a recessionary "trading-down" effect causing high-end luxury shoppers at stores such as Louis Vuitton and Gucci to trade down to Coach—and this will materially impact holiday sales at the retailer.

3. The long lines at the checkout counter of my local Coach store are representative of checkout lines at other Coach stores throughout the country—the result of discounting that will *not* materially impact holiday sales at the retailer.

4. The long lines at the checkout counter of my local Coach store are representative of checkout lines at other Coach

stores throughout the country—the result of regular and expected holiday store traffic, which will *not* materially impact holiday sales at the retailer.

5. The long lines at the checkout counter of my local Coach store are not representative of checkout lines at other Coach stores throughout the country and therefore will *not* materially impact holiday sales at the retailer.

Remember, the best time to buy a company's stock is when you think you know something game-changing about that company that is not yet known by others. The way we do this is by making observations and testing hypotheses. For an observation to qualify as a worthwhile information arbitrage investment, it must lead to a single hypothesis that is (1) game changing—i.e., something that will impact sales, revenue, or profit at a publicly traded company—and (2) not accepted as fact by Wall Street.

Of the five possible hypotheses I constructed for Coach, only two (hypotheses 1 and 2) could potentially be considered game-changing information that could positively impact the company's sales. Just as scientists use lab experiments to test the merits of their scientific hypotheses, I applied investigative research techniques to build a case for or against each of the five possible Coach investment hypotheses to determine which, if any, were correct.

TESTING YOUR HYPOTHESES

My wife, Amy, and I are big fans of investigative crime shows such as *Criminal Minds*, *The Mentalist*, and *CSI: Miami*. We have long wondered why the investigators on these shows insist on examining interior crime scenes in near-total darkness, seeking out clues and evidence by the light of micro-size flashlights when they could simply turn on the lights. Amy was of the opinion that they do this so as not to "disturb" the crime scene with light. I always assumed this was written into the script simply for dramatic affect.

I held that belief until a real-life crime scene investigator revealed to me that a concentrated beam of a directional light helps to focus sight and attention on one small area at a time, while at the same time creating angular shadows that help to reveal evidence one might otherwise overlook in daylight. The controlled, narrow field of vision hides surrounding items that could bias the investigator's perception of evidence.

When determining the validity of your hypotheses it is important that you, like the TV investigators with their flashlights, take steps to make certain that personal predispositions do not derail your ability to scrutinize and interpret impartially the evidence you uncover. You might think Crocs are unsightly, that designer jeans are a poor use of money, or that video games are responsible for the decay of society. But, regardless of your demographic, you are representative of only a small slice of the global consumer market. Your ability to capitalize on information imbalances is directly contingent upon your willingness to view the world as it actually is, not how you see it or how you would like it to be.

Many of the most financially lucrative information arbitrage investment opportunities are created out of biases that exist on Wall Street. If you share in Wall Street's preconceptions, or lack the vision to see around them, your ability to notice the information imbalance will be negated. The trick is to become less self-observant and more observant of those around you.

An important first step in probing your hypotheses for holes is to replicate your initial investment observation—if need be, working in tandem with people in your personal, business, and social networks. In the days following my initial observation at the Coach store in my local mall, I personally visited a dozen Coach stores across North Texas and, thanks to family, friends, and colleagues who assisted me in my efforts, I was able to collect reports of customer traffic at checkout counters for nearly a dozen additional stores in six states.

For each Coach store observation, I recorded and compared the number of shoppers waiting in the checkout line against the number of shoppers waiting in line at competing stores nearby. The accumulated evidence was convincing. Nearly every Coach store visited by me or one of the people helping me in my network had lines spilling out the front door of the store. This was in comparison to the "ghost town" conditions observed at adjoining retailers. My observations were in sync with Web chatter I came across while reading fashion and apparel Web blogs and further verified by store checks conducted by self-directed Coach investors sharing information on investing message boards online.

It did not take long for me to validate as true the partial hypothesis statement: The long lines at the checkout counter of my local Coach store are representative of checkout lines at other Coach stores throughout the country. This finding enabled me to eliminate hypothesis five:

5. The long lines at the checkout counter of my local Coach store are not representative of checkout lines at other Coach stores throughout the country and therefore will *not* materially impact holiday sales at the retailer.

One down, four to go.

In just a few days of visiting malls in my spare time, and with a little help from family, friends, and the Internet, I had successfully replicated my initial observation. But to determine if what I was seeing was truly game changing for the retailer, I had to validate or reject each of the remaining four hypotheses. This would require that I understand the underlying context, the "why" behind those unusually long checkout lines. Only then would the single true hypothesis reveal itself and explain the mystery of the long lines at Coach.

I had so far proven the long lines to be something other than an anomaly. Much in the same way that Horatio Caine, David Caruso's character on *CSI: Miami,* revisits the scene of the crime upon acquisition of newfound knowledge, my quest to reveal the smoking gun behind my newly confirmed observation took me back through the front doors of Coach.

Retail store clerks spend their days working six-to-eight-hour shifts in confined spaces. Their universe is comprised of three things: merchandise, customers, and brain-dulling store music. I can attest to this as a former part-time employee at The Gap. Few have a better read on a retailer's state of affairs than those who work day in and day out on the retailer's front lines. Because corporate management is rarely interested in hearing anything these front-line workers have to say, the workers are typically willing, if not eager, to share everything they know with you. You simply have to ask.

ME: The store is packed today. Is it normal to have such long register lines this time of year?

COACH STORE CLERK: No. I've been working at this store for three years. It's been crazy lately.

ME: Has it been like this through the entire holiday season?

COACH STORE CLERK: Pretty much.

ME: Wow! Congrats, I think. So are you crushing your sales targets?

COACH STORE CLERK: I'm doing okay. We're definitely selling more this holiday season, but the average purchase size is down. I guess that's to be expected in this economy.

ME: Why is that? Is it that people are just going for sale handbags?

COACH STORE CLERK: No, more like in place of handbags people are going for our jewelry and accessories. They love the value-oriented price points.

With very little variation, this conversation repeated itself many times over the ensuing days. As it turned out, none of my five hypotheses had been correct.

The recession had indeed been causing people to trade down, as widely reported in the press, but in the case of Coach, the trading-down effect did not involve buyers of more expensive luxury retailers trading down to Coach products, but Coach's own customers trading down from expensive Coach handbags to lower-priced Coach accessories such as bracelets, wallets, and fragrances—and lots of them.

When taking the recession into account, Coach was fortunate to have customers lining up to buy anything. However, lackluster sales of premium-priced handbags would more than likely counterbalance any increase in revenue the retailer realized from the sale of lower-priced accessories. This was a "bad news, good news" situation for Coach. It was not the game-changing information I was hoping to uncover. The absence of such information therefore disqualified Coach as an information arbitrage investment opportunity. I constructed a new hypothesis, number six, to provide a correct explanation for my Coach observation.

6. The long lines at the checkout counter of my local Coach store are representative of checkout lines at other Coach stores throughout the country—the result of a recessionary "trading-down" effect causing Coach shoppers to "trade down" from higher-priced Coach handbags to less expensive Coach accessories, which will *not* materially impact holiday sales at the retailer.

The Coach example demonstrates the importance of keeping an open mind throughout the investigative due diligence process—something to which any fan of *CSI: Miami,* with its many plot twists, can attest. This investigative journey will take you in directions you would never have imagined possible. Keeping an open mind made it possible for me to discover the one true hypothesis, even though it was one I hadn't initially considered a possibility.

Months later, Coach publicly reported that the company had had decent holiday season sales—not great, but not terrible, either. Upon the release of their holiday sales and earnings report, it was revealed that their stock price did not move significantly in either direction, which reaffirmed that it hadn't been a suitable information arbitrage investment.

While listening to the company's publicly broadcast investor conference call, I was taken aback to learn how dead accurate my in-store interviews had been. During the investor call, Michael Tucci, Coach's North American retail president, commented, "We actually converted [shoppers to buyers] at a much higher rate [which explains the long checkout lines], although at a lower average transaction size or ticket than we saw last year as some consumers were definitely trading down to lower-priced items [just what the store clerks were telling me] . . . new items such as our $98 capacity wristlet were top sellers, while new categories such as jewelry and fragrances were great giftables at sharp prices . . . we did see handbag penetration in our retail stores decline slightly in favor of these lower price point items."

None of what he said should have come as a surprise to me, and not just because of what I learned from the Coach store clerks. That holiday season I finally found and purchased the perfect watch for my wife at—where else? Coach.

GAME-CHANGING INFORMATION

The days spent conducting investigative due diligence on the Coach opportunity was far from a waste of time. Working your way through dead-end observations is an important exercise that will help you recognize the truly game-changing observations that drive successful information arbitrage investments.

One such winning investment of mine involved the youth apparel retailer Urban Outfitters. In the early 2000s the company had perfectly timed the transgression of street attire from the inner city to America's suburbs. What started out as an in-store register-line observation eerily similar to the one I made at Coach resulted in a very different final hypothesis centered on a trend-breaking, game-changing clothing and accessories line that triggered a significant increase in sales at the company. Make enough observations, write and test enough hypotheses, and it will be a matter not of *if* but of *when* and *how often* you successfully uncover the game-changing information that precedes worthwhile information arbitrage investments. The challenge is in learning how to tell the difference between those investment observations that are inconsequential and those that are truly game changing.

In the late 1990s, the combo TV/DVD player was an evolutionary product invention that sold well but had a relatively small financial impact on the large consumer electronics manufacturers and retailers that comprise the industry. The creation of high-definition television, on the other hand, was a game changer that led tens of millions of consumers to purchase new, more expensive television sets over a relatively short period of time. From Samsung to Best Buy, the HD revolution had a material financial impact on dozens of publicly traded companies.

Suppose you are about to read the results of a house inspection for the home of your dreams. A loose gutter or cracked lighting fixture is not going to change your mind about buying the home, but what about news of a costly structural foundation issue or mold problems? That is game-changing news; it will impact your purchase decision. Similarly, for purposes of investing in the stock market, information becomes game changing *when it has the potential to materially impact a company's sales.*

To move the price of a company's stock, the impact on sales must be significant enough to be noticed by the company's investors. The larger the company, the harder it is to "move the needle," so it is not uncommon that information that would be game changing for a small company may not be game changing for a large company. For example, in 2005, Hurricane Katrina nearly pushed the century-old food company Zatarain's—the famous New Orleans–based manufacturer of Cajun-style seasonings—to a manufacturing standstill, causing a negative impact of earnings for its parent company, McCormick & Co. Yet for Kraft, one of the world's largest food companies, with multiple food plants located in the areas affected by the hurricane, the storm was not nearly as detrimental, thanks in part to the company's geographically dispersed workforce and manufacturing capacity. Both companies were impacted by the hurricane, but for the smaller Zatarain's, the impact was game changing.

A single song, even one that becomes a top billboard hit, such as Katy Perry's "Waking Up in Vegas," is unlikely to drive enough business to a tourist destination as diverse and large as Vegas to create a noticeable impact on room vacancy. Likewise, Louis Roederer, the parent company behind Cristal champagne, was not materially impacted by Jay-Z and the hip-hop community's embrace of its flagship product. Cristal is produced in extremely limited quantities, and Louis Roederer has little new upside to gain by the hip-hop world's embracing a product that has been selling out year after year for decades. The vineyards and soil that produce Cristal are some of the finest in the world, making it unfeasible for the company simply to expand its production without jeopardizing the brand's integrity. On the other hand, eighties rap group Run-DMC proved that, however unlikely, it is possible for a single song to become a game changer for even the largest of companies. The first of their genre to reach platinum sales, Run-DMC provided a much-needed boost to the flailing Adidas brand with their 1986 hit song "My Adidas"—so much so, in fact, that the brand went on to offer the group a lucrative sponsorship deal. For Adidas, Run-DMC's hit song was undoubtedly a game changer.

If a single song can move the needle of a multinational consumer products brand, can a film do the same? Yes and no. According to published research from ACNielsen, sales of Pinot Noir did indeed surge more than 16 percent just days after the national release of the film *Sideways*. In the months following, sales of the wine went up by as much as 50 percent. These positive effects were reaffirmed four years later in a report issued by Sonoma State University and Sonoma Research Associates.

Yet the movie had an immaterial impact on consolidated sales among the publicly traded global wine and liquor companies, due to the sheer size and diversity of their product lines. To the large beverage companies dealing in sales of wine, beer, and liquor, the film's effect on the sale of Pinot Noir was not a game changer, but another, less obvious company, while not at all involved in sales of Pinot Noir, stood to benefit as much or more from the film than any winery.

I got married the same month as the film's premier, and that meant that most of my weekends leading up to the film's release were spent picking out items for our wedding registry—boring household stuff such as bed linens, towels, and flatware. Oh, and wineglasses. Was it be possible that our trip to the movie theater and our wedding registry shopping trips could result in a winning information arbitrage investment?

A year after the film's release, wineglass manufacturer Riedel reported a 50 percent increase in North American sales, largely due to an increase in demand for its Pinot Noir glasses. Unfortunately, Riedel was not at the time publicly traded—the ultimate deal breaker for any information arbitrage investment, and the very first thing an investor should verify prior to beginning investigative due diligence.

I learned that lesson the hard way while observing the global reemergence of dance sparked by competitive dance shows on TV.

I had taken the time to phone-interview dance studio managers, excitedly confirming excessive waiting lists for kids' hip-hop and Bollywood dance classes across eight states, before learning that the dance apparel company Danskin was no longer a publicly traded company. That is a mistake I will never repeat. Never spin your wheels on due diligence research unless you have first identified a publicly traded company in a position either to benefit or be negatively impacted from the game-changing information you have uncovered.

The beautiful Italian landscapes and inspirational life message of the 2003 runaway hit film *Under the Tuscan Sun* caused a notable spike in Italian tourism. The problem was, as in the case of *Sideways*, I was unable to find any publicly traded companies that stood to benefit from the film's unique portrayal of life in Italy. I would not be surprised if Italy's board of tourism had to staff up in the months after the film's release to handle the country's newfound popularity—unfortunately for me, it is not possible to purchase stock in government-run tourist bureaus.

It didn't take long, though, for me to find a publicly traded company that stood to benefit from James Cameron's 2009 epic 3D blockbuster film *Avatar*. Before my friends and I had even left the theater, I turned to them and said two things: "We've just witnessed the future of filmed entertainment" and "We should have seen this at the IMAX." I knew that the stunning visuals of this 3D film—and all the 3D films that were sure to follow in the wake of its success—would usher in a new era of high-budget visual masterpieces ideally suited for IMAX's super-size domed screens. *Avatar* and the 3D revolution in filmed entertainment were sure to be game changers for the publicly traded oversize-screen movie operator IMAX.

And indeed, in the months following the film's release, the company's stock price would climb over 60 percent. While announcing record quarterly box office revenue and profits that were more than double the company's prior record, IMAX CEO Rich Gelfond said, "Obviously that was positively impacted by *Avatar*."

Where *Avatar* took just three hours to change the way in which we, as a society, consumed filmed entertainment in public, Netflix took nearly a decade to change the way we consumed filmed entertainment in our home. While this change in consumer behavior did not happen overnight, the paradigm shift away from in-store video rental and toward mail-based and in-home video streaming subscription services was nonetheless a game changer for both publicly traded Netflix and Blockbuster Entertainment. The latter, as a result, was pushed to the brink of bankruptcy. The top line in the following chart represents the historical performance of Netflix stock; the bottom line, Blockbuster stock.

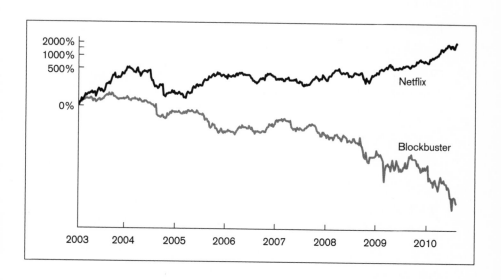

Having spent the prior decade living just a few blocks from a Blockbuster video store, I never had a need to subscribe to Netflix. It is regrettable that I didn't ignore the company only as a customer, but also as an investor. I let my own geographic bias blind me to one of the most widely adopted and game-changing consumer trends of my generation.

At the peak of the Atkins diet craze, the National Bread Leadership Council released a study claiming a 40 percent drop over a year in American bread consumption—an unequivocal game changer for bakeries. I have vivid memories of this time, as nearly every restaurant I frequented was proudly highlighting their Atkins-friendly low-carb menu items. The widely adopted anti-bread, pro-meat diet severely impacted global commodity prices for bread and beef, while causing havoc for a number of publicly traded companies, none more so than Interstate Bakeries Corp., the Kansas City, Missouri, maker of Wonder bread and Twinkies—who, in September of 2005, filed for bankruptcy. (The company eventually emerged from bankruptcy.)

"Consumer interest in low-carbohydrate diets has contributed to the reduced demand" for Interstate's products, chief financial officer Ronald Hutchison said in court bankruptcy papers. "Consumer interest in reduced carbohydrate consumption increased during the last fiscal year as a result of the popularity of diets such as the Atkins and South Beach diets." Prior to the low-carb diet craze, the company's stock, nearly worthless at the time of the bankruptcy filing, had traded as high as $34.

The movement toward storing cord blood of newborns at $2,000 per child would go on to become a game changer within the medical diagnostics industry—so much so that the billion-dollar medical-diagnostics giant PerkinElmer would eventually pay nearly double the going share price to acquire the publicly traded cord blood company ViaCell in 2007. I am not convinced that storing cord blood has potential to provide any real medical benefit, yet at this very moment the cord blood of our recently born son and daughter is being stored at subzero temperatures at a ViaCell facility. I suspect the annual payments I reluctantly make to ViaCell will continue for years.

Probably the biggest game changer in the world of fast food was Wendy's decision to launch a health-conscious line of Garden Sensations salads. Nearly overnight my wife, who was never one to patronize fast-food restaurants, became a repeat Wendy's customer. She was not the only one. The Chicken BLT, Mandarin Chicken, Spring Mix, and Taco Supremo salads would go on to become among the best-selling and most profitable items on Wendy's menu, fueling a rise in sales, profits, and stock price for the fast-food innovation leader.

When does a video game become game changing? When your retirement-age boss and preteen niece play the game with as much enthusiasm as a sixteen-year-old boy. The game Guitar Hero has become a cultural phenomenon by enabling players with no musical training to mimic the experience of "rocking out" to their favorite hits via a simulated guitar-shaped game controller. Activision, the maker of Guitar Hero, saw its stock nearly triple while selling twenty-five million copies—that's $2 billion. I'm not sure which memories I cherish more: my Guitar Hero investment profits or the fun I had conducting due diligence on the product.

Must-have fashion items seem to pop up weekly in trendy coastal cities such as New York and Los Angeles. But it's the trends that soccer moms and their children across Middle America embrace that are most likely to become game changers for the apparel companies that sell them. Ugg boots, True Religion jeans, and Crocs sandals are three game-changing fashion trends that took Middle America by storm. From Tulsa, Oklahoma, to Dayton, Ohio, you will find these companies' boots, jeans, and sandals in the closets of tens of millions of consumers.

I often refer to these three products as the triple crown of fashion investing. As little as $1,000 invested in Ugg's parent company, Decker, in late 2002 (that's roughly the cost of five pairs of Ugg boots), parlayed into True Religion stock in early 2004, and again parlayed into the stock of Crocs shortly after the company's IPO in February of 2006, would have grown to $750,000 by 2007. That's 750 times your money in just five years. Think of all the pairs of designer jeans that would buy!

Trends that infiltrate the workplace can be just as game changing as those that impact consumers. When you work for a large Fortune 1000 company that switches shipping vendors from Federal Express to UPS, or computing vendors from Dell to Hewlett-Packard, that is not a game-changing event for any of the parties concerned. But when your stodgy, old, bureaucratic company embraces change to adopt the product or technology of a new start-up vendor you've never heard of, it is time to take notice.

Chances are good that you or someone you know worked for one of the tens of thousands of companies this past decade who ditched their legacy CRM software platform for the cheaper, Web-based Salesforce.com, a game-changing corporate trend causing the price of the Salesforce's stock to climb sixfold, from $15 to $90, in the six years since its IPO.

Sometimes game-changing moments are the product of geo-political events. The events of 9/11 were as game changing as any in recent American history. Among other things, the terrorist attacks triggered a renewed focus on security at airports around the world. Those perceptive enough to purchase shares of Invision, a leading publicly traded bomb-detection-equipment company, on September 11, 2001, were rewarded with an investment return of nearly ten times their money just one year later.

In January of 2009, just weeks before taking office, U.S. president-elect Barack Obama pledged to dispense $50 billion to doctors and hospitals to subsidize the purchase of software systems, with the goal of computerizing the health records of all Americans within five years. If you are one of the handful of companies selling healthcare record-keeping software, this is game-changing information. The stock price of Cerner Corporation, one of the largest such companies, would more than double over the ten-month period following the president's promise.

Game-changing information can be found anywhere, anytime—from the office to the mall to the security checkpoint at the airport. You could stumble across game-changing information at a fast-food drive-through window, at a movie theater, while flipping through tabloid magazines, or while watching a presidential speech on TV. The scientific model of making observations and testing hypotheses will help you to confidently determine if the game-changing information you identify is likely to have a material impact on the sales of a publicly traded company.

7

YOU KNOW SOMETHING THEY DON'T

Outsmarting Wall Street's Brightest

The journey from making an observation to making an investment involves two steps. The first step is to devise, test, and prove true a game-changing investment hypothesis. You should now know how to do that. The second step is to verify that Wall Street is unaware of or ill informed about your game-changing discovery. For this final step, your chances for success are greatest when you focus on opportunities that Wall Street is most likely to miss.

Fortunately for you, no professional involved in predictive analysis, regardless of his field of specialty, is correct 100 percent of the time. Whatever level of predictive accuracy that does exist among Wall Street professionals tends to decline in proportion to the lack of perceived importance of the subject matter under discussion or debate. The reason for this is simple: the laws of economics dictate that the best and brightest focus their energies on opportunities where the most is at stake.

For example, in the world of media, international events such as devastating natural disasters demand and receive the best in unbiased, high-quality journalism and in-depth reporting, while local or niche events impacting fewer people are far more likely to suffer from spotty, inaccurate media coverage.

In the high-stakes game of oil exploration, Exxon, with its army of A-list geologists and cutting-edge technology, is far less likely to lose $100 million drilling a dry well in Saudi Arabia than the aspiring Texas oilman and his nephew "geologist-in-training" who are drilling shallow wildcat wells outside Houston.

In the scientific field of astronomy, small meteorites routinely enter our atmosphere unnoticed, making novel souvenirs for the Iowa farmers who stumble across their remnants. But should the doomsday asteroid ever threaten to extinguish the human species, you can bet we'll receive some degree of advance warning from astronomers tripping over themselves to claim the discovery.

The more there is to gain or lose, the more likely the "professionals" are to get it right. This suggests that the lion's share of investment opportunities to discover information imbalances lies with smaller, little-known companies. Supporting this theory are the previously cited comparisons between professionally managed mutual funds and unmanaged index funds. These comparisons clearly show that the greatest margin of professional underperformance coincides with professionally managed funds targeting small companies.

Hansen Natural Corporation, the California-based beverage giant known for its natural sodas, fruit juices, and Monster energy drinks, was not too long ago a small company and one of the most underestimated stocks on Wall Street. The company, which had an odd history of refusing to issue earnings forecasts to Wall Street analysts, was one of only a handful of publicly traded stocks without an investor relations department. As a result, just three investment firms on Wall Street assigned analysts to cover and write investment opinions on Hansen's stock. Hansen CEO Rodney C. Sacks is famous for saying that amateur stock message boards offer "the best research that can be done," including analysis by actual customers who visit stores to check Hansen products' shelf presence. From 2003 through 2006, Hansen's stock price rose more than sixtyfold, from $2 to over $120, making it one of the best performing stocks of the decade. During this period the company was largely off Wall Street's radar. Many of those who reaped the financial rewards of Hansen's success were not Wall Street insiders but small investors who were regular consumers of the company's products.

So, all else being equal, you can assume that the discovery of game-changing information involving small companies is more likely to coincide with an information imbalance than the discovery of game-changing information involving large companies. This makes the story of one of my most successful and longest running information arbitrage investments so intriguing, as it involves the stock of a company that is, by anyone's measure, one of the world's largest and most well known, generating annual revenue in excess of $50 billion.

The company's business is regularly dissected by both the Wall Street press corps and teams of senior analysts at more than forty of Wall Street's largest and most prestigious investment firms. Many consider the company to be the most widely covered and overanalyzed on Wall Street. Yet fiscal quarter after fiscal quarter, for years on end, the innate biases of those on Wall Street have caused the professionals to grossly underestimate consumer interest in this company's products—resulting in one colossal information imbalance after another.

Chances are that you're familiar, if not intimately acquainted, with the products made by the company I'm referring to. Its name is Apple.

All my life, I have been a "PC guy." Beginning in high school and throughout every corporate job I've ever held, my only exposure to computing has been working on PCs. And like a lot of people, I tend to resist unnecessary change, especially if that change requires me to learn new things. Combine that with Apple's premium price points for Mac computers—and the fear that change will not improve my livelihood but will, instead, cause me to have to learn a new way of doing things—and you start to understand my reluctance to change my PC ways.

For many years this was the norm in my world. Other than the sole Web site designer at my former company, to my knowledge not a single person in my family, social, or business network owned a Mac. The first person I knew of to "go Mac" was a longtime friend by the name of Len Critcher. Len, being a semiprofessional videographer, purchased his Mac specifically for its unique video editing capabilities, which seemed to make sense.

But then something weird started to happen. He started to talk about his Mac *a lot*, in a really annoying way, and not in a way I had ever heard anyone talk about his computer. He had become obsessed with how great his Mac was for every imaginable use. But he also began to ask an irritating question: "How do you antiquated barbarians possibly get through the day using a PC?" Okay, he wasn't that blunt, but it wasn't as if he hadn't been getting by on a PC just fine his entire life up to that point.

Over time this peculiar behavior escalated to a point where he could no longer sit through a friendly lunch or dinner without instigating an unwelcome Mac vs. PC debate. Before long, several in our circle raised the red flag of defeat, trading in their PCs for Macs—and were rewarded by no longer having to bear the brunt of Len's "You're missing out on life because you don't use a Mac" lectures. Soon after, I watched as, like a row of tipping dominos, each and every one of my friends made the switch from a PC to a Mac.

Len was first, then Dave, Jerry, Jason, Drew, Jordan, Brett, Blaine, Merritt, and, yes, eventually even I reluctantly bought a MacBook to use as our family computer at home. Even then, though, I resisted *using* the Mac, sticking to my company-issued laptop PC (which I held onto through three batteries, two keyboard replacements, and a near-fatal hard drive crash requiring multiple days of data reconstruction by my company's IT team). As I said, I can be really stubborn when it comes to instituting change in my life. That was, until the day I saw the light of Apple for myself. That day, we were launching a youth-focused research panel at my company in which we needed to determine which brands of gift cards to offer as program rewards. We were seeking incentives that were most likely to entice teens and young adults to participate in market research surveys. As part of our research efforts, I moderated a focus group comprised of young consumers age fourteen through twenty-five. I solicited feedback on gift card reward options spanning a multitude of categories, ranging from youth apparel stores to fast-food dining certificates.

Opinions were fairly mixed, until I floated the idea of Apple gift cards. This suggestion invoked an emotional response unlike any other I had witnessed from a focus group—before or since. The tired young faces in the room lit up in exhilaration at the mere idea of being able to earn gift cards toward Apple products. Those who did not own a Mac computer wanted one, and those who already had a Mac either desired a newer model or had an interest in other Apple devices, accessories, or music downloads through the company's iTunes store.

The high price of Apple products did not seem to deter their long-ing to own the brand's products. It wasn't designer clothing or fancy cars they craved, but "Apple this, Apple that." If consumer electron-ics had become the new fashion, Apple was Chanel, Prada, and Ver-sace combined. These young people's loyalty to the Apple brand went uncontested. There was no runner-up, no "nearly as good" second-choice brand of electronic products that would satisfy their unend-ing desire to get their hands on the latest, greatest Apple product.

I pursued follow-up conversations with several of the group's par-ticipants, seeking to better understand the driving force behind the seemingly hypnotic influence the Apple brand had over them. Through my conversations, it became clear how, unlike the genera-tions before them, who viewed computers as tools of productivity, to-day's youth, thanks in part to the evolution of social networking sites such as Facebook, viewed computers as private gateways connect-ing all aspects of their most personal endeavors. They were their 24/7 portholes to laughter, tears, friendship, and love—a place to reveal and broadcast their inner selves to the world.

Computers and computer-like devices had become this new gen-eration's window to life. To them, the computer had become much more of a pleasure-oriented than a work-oriented device. Only by recognizing the emotional imprint of such "computing-centric" expe-riences can one understand why a teenager earning minimum wage would enthusiastically save up hundreds of dollars and make lifestyle trade-offs in order to be able to afford what she perceived to be a supe-rior, though premium-priced, computer from Apple.

Now I was eager to experience the Apple hype firsthand. I went home that evening and, in the days that followed, forced myself to use our family MacBook instead of my laptop PC. I quickly recog-nized that everything about the Mac—the sleek design, the simple, user-friendly operating system, the soft-set texture of the mouse and keyboard, the micro-size magnetic power connector, the feel of its solidly crafted construction in my hands and on my lap—enhanced what was a very pleasurable and personal user experience. This was a complete contrast to the cold and clinical impression I got while using my laptop PC.

All things visual, whether it was video or digital photographs, looked better on the Mac—much the way clothing looks better in the mirror of a perfectly lit dressing room. Many of the things that made the Mac experience so wonderful cannot be easily explained. To those who use them (and that number grows daily), Macs just seem to feel better, look better, and work better.

When it comes to a product you use more than any other in your life, a small amount of "better" can be very meaningful. Following the trail blazed by those before me, I soon found that Apple had stolen my heart and seized control of my wallet.

I remember the day I called Len to tell him how right he had been, and to thank him for his part in introducing me to the world of Apple. As with my undying preference for drinking Coke, it was now hard for me to imagine a time in the future when I wouldn't be a customer of Apple. And while I would never allow myself to demonize the PC users in my life (as had previously been done to me), I occasionally did catch myself using words such as *incredible, amazing, fantastic, unbelievable, beautiful, stunning, awesome,* and even *magical* when describing Apple products.

Over the years my observations surrounding the all-encompassing consumer appetite for Apple products have led me to devise, test, and prove true many game-changing investment hypotheses, all of which now seem quite obvious in the wake of Apple's rampant global success. But Wall Street has greeted each new Apple product release with a cloud of doubt and negativity, as reflected by years of missed earnings estimates by its top analysts. And the financial pages have warned us of Apple's imminent collapse, even while the company's bond with consumers has grown stronger. Whether it was with regard to the MacBook, iPod, iPhone, or iPad, Wall Street was oblivious to the paradigm shift taking place in how millions of consumers had begun to engage with their computing devices—and the impact that this change would have on their purchasing behavior.

This oversight fed an atmosphere of bewilderment and doubt on Wall Street related to Apple's capacity to sustain its record success with each new product launch, which, in turn, set the stage for some extraordinarily successful information arbitrage investments.

How is it that Wall Street's brightest could have been so wrong about Apple? You will not find a more disproportionate number of people carrying PCs and BlackBerrys (in comparison to Macs and iPhones) anywhere on earth than on the streets of New York's Financial District. This is the epicenter of the business world and the one market, for better or worse, that Apple has for years ignored. Wall Street's male-dominated, straight-and-narrow, all-things-business mind-set; geographic seclusion from mainstream America; and detached, impersonal view of the computing and mobile phone industries comprised a perfect storm of bias fueling its unfounded skepticism of the touchy-feely and emotionally driven Apple brand.

This skepticism impaired Wall Street's ability to see and acknowledge the magnitude of the authentic connection Apple had been organically garnering with a new generation of consumers. Unlike those from prior generations, these consumers were much more interested in user experience than product features. While Apple was winning over the hearts and minds of tens of millions of consumers around the globe, Wall Street remained distracted with concerns about the

MacBook's nonremovable battery, the iPod's premium price points, the inferior music encryption quality on iTunes, the iPhone's lack of a physical keyboard, and the iPad's inability to display content requiring Flash players. Every newly launched Apple product was discredited with a laundry list of its "indispensable" missing features and the lower-priced competing products set to trigger Apple's inevitable demise.

Be it netbooks, me-too digital media players, or the ever-rotating "iPhone killer" of the month, there has never been a shortage of cheaper, fuller-featured alternatives to compete with Apple products. Yet a thousand Wall Street analysts comparing and contrasting price points and product features while sifting through one another's research reports and the product reviews of socially sheltered technology columnists will fail to notice or appreciate the business impact of Emily, an eleven-year-old doing the happy dance while holding her first iPod touch; or the brimming smile of Susan, a technology-averse mom using the iPhone4's FaceTime to look into the eyes of her daughter at college two thousand miles away; or Beth, a sixty-year-old bookworm gloating about her magical new iPad to members of her weekly book club.

No stack of spreadsheets or charts can account for the hundreds of Apple devices these three unlikely product evangelists will help sell simply by sharing their spine-tingling life experiences with family, friends, or that curious onlooker sipping coffee beside them at Starbucks. Emily, Susan, and Beth—and millions of jubilant Apple fans just like them—are the single most important part of the Apple success story. Yet, from the invention of the iPod to the evolution of the iPad, you would be challenged to find a single mention of anyone like Emily, Susan, or Beth in any Wall Street analyst's report or professional investment opinion on Apple.

Week of July 4, 2007

The original Apple iPhone is released in the United States; Apple's stock price: $122.

A few days after the summer launch of the first-generation iPhone, my wife and I just happened to be hosting our annual Fourth of July pool party, so it was not surprising to have several friends arrive proudly sporting their shiny new iPhones. Just five minutes experiencing the device firsthand was all it took for me to dethrone the digital video recorder (DVR) and replace it with the iPhone as my new favorite greatest invention of all time.

My feelings were not unique. Excited attention was deservedly centered on the iPhones as they were passed around and marveled at by everyone at the party. One thing was clear. For the vast majority of our guests that day, it was not a question of *if* but *when* they would be buying their own iPhones. Nearly every one of our friends and neighbors expressed one of the following three sentiments: (1) I intend to buy an iPhone tomorrow; (2) I intend to buy an iPhone once my existing mobile phone contract expires; or (3) I intend to buy an iPhone once the price drops to some predetermined dollar amount I have in my head as the maximum amount of money I am willing to spend on a mobile phone.

The impact of this observation can be appreciated fully only when you take into account how, just hours earlier, few if any of these new prospective Apple customers had given serious consideration to buying an iPhone. Over the coming days I would replicate this observation while speaking with a broader group of family, neighbors, friends, and coworkers—while also reading hundreds of spontaneous Internet postings from *real* people on community blogs and Web sites (not technology review sites) discussing in detail their first hands-on experience with the iPhone, along with their intention to own one for themselves. My direct observations led me to devise, test, and prove true the following game-changing hypothesis:

Hypothesis. As with the iPod before it, most people (regardless of age or sex) who come into direct contact with an iPhone come to view it as a life-changing device that they instantly desire to own. This infectious emotional reaction will contribute to unprecedented viral and word-of-mouth marketing for the product, which will cause iPhone to become one of the world's top-selling mobile phones and Apple to become one of the world's leading manufacturers of mobile phones, which will have a material positive impact on Apple's revenue.

Now that I was convinced of my game-changing hypothesis, I had to make certain that the hypothesis was not widely known or accepted as fact by Wall Street (confirming that "what I know" is something "they don't know").

SEEING THINGS FROM WALL STREET'S POINT OF VIEW

Up until now, your potential investing success has hinged upon circumventing the opinions of investment "experts"; leveraging information uncovered through your own life, social network, and the Internet; and applying unconventional investigative due diligence techniques to measure firsthand the pulse of the products and companies that shape great investments. But the only way to ascertain that "what you know" is indeed something "they don't know" is to assess your game-changing hypothesis from the viewpoint of those you are trying to outwit: the Wall Street investment professionals, the mainstream financial press, and the investors who follow their lead.

Seeing things from a "Wall Street" point of view requires that you wipe your slate clean of everything you have observed and learned that supports your investment hypothesis. Beginning with a blank slate, you will now seek out any and all public information supporting or opposing your game-changing hypothesis. You will do this by exclusively using the information channels that are widely available to Wall Street professionals and those traditional investors who rely on their advice.

By being astutely observant, unbiased, and unconventional, you have constructed an investment hypothesis based on game-changing information. But only by viewing your investment hypothesis through the biased and narrowly focused field of vision that is all too often the norm on Wall Street will you be able to confirm or deny the existence of an information imbalance.

You will find this final stage to be the most straightforward part of the investigative due diligence process. No more in-store interviews, late-night digging through obscure blogs and Internet forum postings, or need to extract knowledge from your personal and business social networks. Unlike the hypothesis-testing phase of the investigative due diligence process, ascertaining the existence of an information imbalance can be done in just one to two days using a single Web site.

Yahoo! Finance (finance.yahoo.com) is the world's leading finance site. Type any company name or stock symbol into the Get Quotes field on Yahoo! Finance and you will find a consolidated history of company earnings, conference calls, news stories, and analyst reports compiled from nearly all of the world's most prestigious business news distribution services and publications. Thanks to the development of the Internet and the passing of Regulation FD (Full

Disclosure) by the Securities and Exchange Commission in 2000, today even the smallest of us self-directed investors have at our fingertips instant access to the same company information previously made available only to large institutional investors and investment firms. This makes today's Wall Street an open book.

To find out "what they know" simply requires reading what "they" read and write. And while many investment firms still disclose their proprietary company analyst reports only to clients, the underlying theme of the analyst's position in the report is nearly always broadcast and reprinted in multiple forms of mass-published financial media that can be found on Yahoo! Finance. Your job is to read each and every published analyst report, news story, and financial blog dating back six months that pertains to the company for which you have developed your game-changing hypothesis.

When available, you should also read the transcript or listen to a taped record of the most recent company-broadcasted earnings conference call (available on many company Web sites), paying special close attention to the analyst question-and-answer portion of the call. Your game-changing hypothesis should not comprise any financial or numerical data, so it is not necessary—and it can even be detrimental—for you to pay attention to financial data or financial speak contained in your readings.

Skip over any and all mention of or reference to financial or technical analysis in your readings. You are interested in only the comments and opinions directly related to your investment hypothesis.

As you read and listen, compile two separate lists of quotations— List A will contain analyst and journalist quotes that *support* the focal point of your hypothesis. List B will contain analyst and journalist quotes that *reject* the focal point of your hypothesis. The compiling and sorting of quotes is, to a high degree, subjective, so it is important that you zero in on the focal point of your hypothesis (the one component of your hypothesis that is game changing) that, if true, will be responsible for the material revenue impact you are predicting.

So, again, here is my overall hypothesis regarding the Apple iPhone:

Hypothesis. As with the iPod before it, most people (regardless of age or sex) who come into direct contact with an iPhone come to view it as a life-changing device that they instantly desire to own. This infectious emotional reaction will contribute to unprecedented viral and word-of-mouth marketing for the product, which will cause iPhone to become one of the world's top-selling mobile phones and Apple to become one of the world's leading manufacturers of mobile phones, which will have a material positive impact on Apple's revenue.

The focal point of my hypothesis is "iPhone to become one of the world's top-selling mobile phones." With that focal point in mind, journalist and analyst quotes in the vein of "The iPhone is sure to become a worldwide phenomenon" and "Watch out, Nokia and BlackBerry—Apple's iPhone set to shake up if not dominate the mobile phone industry" would be placed on List A.

Quotes such as "All hype, no substance—the iPhone will fail," "Apple's goals for iPhone seem ambitious," and "Apple and iPhone to face an uphill battle" would be placed on List B. Quotes such as "The iPhone is a breakthrough handheld computer," "The phone's Edge network is dreadfully slow," and "It rocks!," which do not specifically support or reject the underlying focal point of my hypothesis, would not be included on either list.

When compiling these quotes, be sure to include a reference to each quote's original source. No single analyst or journalist should contribute more than one quote to each of your two lists, unless the timing of their quotes is more than thirty days apart. Upon completion of this exercise, separately add up the number of quotes in List A and List B.

On the off chance that List A does not have any quotes, congratulations! You have just uncovered a very strong information imbalance. If List A has quotes, and List B does not have any quotes, then no information imbalance exists. If both Lists A and B have quotes, divide the total number of quotes on List A by the total number of quotes on List B. The resulting number is what I refer to as a consensus score. The higher the consensus score, the higher the likelihood that Wall Street is already aware of and in agreement with your investment hypothesis, in which case an information imbalance is unlikely. Any consensus score greater than 2 is indicative of information parity— meaning that both you and Wall Street possess the same information.

Any consensus score less than 2 indicates the existence of an information imbalance, with a consensus score less than 0.5 indicative of a strong information imbalance. The closer your consensus score is to zero, the better. While the interpretation of information is highly subjective and not an exact science, I have found the consensus score to be a good tool—one that can help you quantify the level of consensus or uncertainty, with regard to your investment hypothesis, that exists on Wall Street.

Upon conclusion of your investigative due diligence, you will use the consensus score as a guide to determining whether, based on your readings, Wall Street has accepted as fact the focal point of your game-changing hypothesis. The more uncertainty and conflicting opinions you find surrounding your investment hypothesis, the larger the information imbalance. A larger information imbalance will generally equate to a larger jump in stock price once the game-changing information you know to be true reaches a point of information parity on Wall Street.

I repeat the consensus score exercise monthly for each of my active information arbitrage investments, computing an updated score based on published quotes from the prior thirty-day period. The moment the recomputed consensus score climbs above 2 (signifying information parity), I know to exit my position in the investment. This determination to exit an investment—i.e., to sell stock—*is made independent of whether I have made or lost money on the investment.* Having the strength of mind to exit a winning or losing investment at the point at which your game-changing hypothesis reaches information parity is central to becoming a successful information arbitrage investor. Once the information you have identified to be game changing becomes widely accepted as fact by other investors, your first-mover advantage is lost. Shake it off—if need be, take a loss—and refocus your energy on detecting the next game-changing investment opportunity.

Any consensus score *less than 2* indicates the existence of an information imbalance and an opportunity to initiate an information arbitrage investment. Any consensus score *above 2* is indicative of information parity and should be taken as a sign to exit your information arbitrage investment.

Applying this exercise to my game-changing iPhone hypothesis resulted in a consensus score just under 0.5, indicating a strong information imbalance. Reminiscing on Apple's public release of the original iPhone, it might seem hard to believe how any information imbalance could have existed, considering that the iPhone launch probably received as much, if not more, business media attention than any prior product release in U.S. history. Yet, while the iPhone did receive a tremendous amount of positive publicity at launch, nearly every story included a heavy dose of skepticism, be it related to the phone's high price, questionable call quality, or lack of basic features such as a physical keyboard, a removable battery, SMS instant messaging, voice dialing, songs as ringtones, cut and paste, video recording, expandable storage, or Flash support.

But my game-changing iPhone hypothesis, "iPhone to become one of the world's top-selling mobile phones," was one not of floundering uncertainty but of conviction based upon real observations I had seen with my own eyes. And few if any on Wall Street or in the business media, when taking into consideration all the theoretical challenges facing iPhone, were prepared at the time to jump on my "iPhone to become one of the world's top-selling mobile phones" bandwagon.

What follows is an example of the skeptical to downright defiant quotes regarding iPhone that over the years have appeared on my iPhone hypothesis List A:

- "There is no likelihood that Apple can be successful in a business this competitive. . . . If it's smart it will call the iPhone a 'reference design' and pass it to some suckers to build with someone else's marketing budget. Then it can wash its hands of any marketplace failures." (John C. Dvorak, technology columnist for Dow-Jones Marketwatch.com and *PC Magazine*, March 28, 2007)
- "As customers start to realize that the competition offers better functionality at a lower price . . . sales will stagnate.

After a year a new version will be launched, but it will lack the innovation of the first and quickly vanish. The only question remaining is if, when the iPod phone fails, it will take the iPod with it." (Bill Ray, writer for the UK technology site The Register, "Why the Apple Phone Will Fail, and Fail Badly," December 23, 2006)

- "What does the iPhone offer that other cell phones do not already offer, or will offer soon? The answer is not very much ... Apple's stated goal of selling 10 million iPhones by the end of 2008 seems ambitious." (Laura Goldman, money manager at LSG Capital, May 21, 2007)

- "[iPhone] just doesn't matter anymore. There are now alternatives to the iPhone, which has been introduced everywhere else in the world. It's no longer a novelty." (Eamon Hoey, Hoey and Associates, April 30, 2008)

- "Apple is slated to come out with a new phone ... And it will largely fail. . . . Sales for the phone will skyrocket initially. However, things will calm down, and the Apple phone will take its place on the shelves with the random video cameras, cell phones, wireless routers and other would-be hits ... When the iPod emerged in late 2001, it solved some major problems with MP3 players. Unfortunately for Apple, problems like that don't exist in the handset business. Cell phones aren't clunky, inadequate devices. Instead, they are pretty good. Really good." (Michael Kanellos, CNET, December 7, 2006)

- "I am pretty skeptical ... For starters, while Apple basically established the market for portable music players, the phone market is already established, with a number of major brands." (Jack Gold, founder and principal analyst at J. Gold Associates, January 11, 2007)

- "The iPhone is nothing more than a luxury bauble that will appeal to a few gadget freaks. In terms of its impact on the industry, the iPhone is less relevant . . . Apple is unlikely to make much of an impact on this market . . . Apple will sell a few to its fans, but the iPhone won't make a long-term mark on the industry." (Matthew Lynn, Bloomberg, January 15, 2007)

- "The iPhone's willful disregard of the global handset market will come back to haunt Apple." (Tero Kuittinen, Real-Money.com, January 18, 2007)

- "Consumers are not used to paying another couple hundred bucks more just because Apple makes a cool product. Some fans will buy [the iPhone], but for the rest of us it's a hard pill to swallow just to have the coolest thing." (Neil Strother, NPD Group analyst, January 22, 2007)

- "I'm more convinced than ever that, after an initial frenzy of publicity and sales to early adopters, iPhone sales will be unspectacular . . . iPhone may well become Apple's next Newton." (David Haskin, *Computerworld*, February 26, 2007)

- "The iPhone is a bandwidth hog and is not profitable for carriers. Rivals are entering the mobile browser space to compete with Apple. Although Apple's gadgets are trendy, their hardware will eventually become irrelevant." (Edward Zabitsky, analyst with ACI Research, December 29, 2009)

- "You know the beautiful thing: June 29, 2009, is the two-year anniversary of the first shipment of the iPhone. Not one of those people will still be using an iPhone a month later. Think about it—if you bought the first iPhone, you bought it because you wanted the coolest product on the market. Your two-year contract has just expired. Look around. Tell me what they're going to buy." (Roger McNamee, cofounder of Elevation Partners, March 5, 2009)

- "But when it comes right down to it, the BlackBerry Storm will be the superior mobile device and represents a true iPhone killer." (Andrew Hickey, ChannelWeb, November 14, 2008)

- "Apple begins selling its revolutionary iPhone this summer and it will mark the end of the string of hits for the company." (Todd Sullivan, Seeking Alpha, May 15, 2007)

- "The iPhone will not substantially alter the fundamental structure and challenges of the mobile industry." (Charles Golvin, Forrester Research Inc., January 2007)

- "The economics of something like this aren't that compelling." (Rod Bare, Morningstar, December 8, 2006)

- "The iPhone is going to be nothing more than a temporary novelty that will eventually wear off." (Gundeep Hora, editor in chief, CoolTechZone.com, April 7, 2007)

- "iPhone, which doesn't look, I mean to me, I'm looking at this thing and I think it's kind of trending against, you know, what's really going, what people are really liking on, in these phones nowadays, which are those little keypads. I mean, the Blackjack from Samsung, the BlackBerry, obviously, you know kind of pushes this thing, the Palm, all these . . . And I guess some of these stocks went down on the Apple announcement, thinking that Apple could do no wrong, but I think Apple can do wrong and I think this is it." (John C. Dvorak, CBS MarketWatch, January 13, 2007)

- "There's no chance that the iPhone is going to get any significant market share." (Steve Ballmer, Microsoft CEO, February 24, 2009)

Interesting, right? Well, let's skip forward . . .

November 10, 2008
iPhone reported as "Best-Selling Phone in the U.S."

July 6, 2009
iPhone reported as "Best-Selling Smartphone in Japan."

December 15, 2009
iPhone reported as "Best-Selling Phone in Korea."

April 8, 2010
Apple CEO Steve Jobs reports cumulative iPhone sales of fifty million handsets.

June 16, 2010
Apple's stock price is $267. *Bloomberg Businessweek* publishes an article titled "Nokia [the world's largest manufacturer of mobile phones] Lowers Forecasts Amid iPhone Competition."

Information arbitrage investing by its nature means that the best investing opportunities will be those in which you are able to find little to no support for your investment hypothesis. The most difficult obstacle to overcome as a self-directed investor is neglecting to believe in what you observe, independent of the opposing opinions of "investment professionals" or subject matter experts. Once you have developed the confidence to do so, you will find yourself with the willpower to pursue and exploit the information imbalances you discover.

I often reread the iPhone quotes just given, both as a reminder of what is possible and to empower myself to trust my own observations and investigative due diligence over the biased speculation of others when pursuing new information arbitrage investments. Amazingly, it wasn't for several years after iPhone's public launch, only after the indisputable evidence of its success in handset sales had been reported, that Wall Street fully acknowledged iPhone as one of the world's best-selling mobile phones. By the summer of 2010 the number of compiled analyst and journalist quotes supporting the focal point of my iPhone hypothesis (List A) exceeded by a large margin the number of compiled analyst and journalist quotes rejecting the focal point of my iPhone hypothesis (List B). The consensus score had finally climbed above 2, meaning that my game-changing iPhone investment hypothesis had reached a point of information parity.

While the opportunities to uncover information imbalances might be greater for investment hypotheses involving small companies, simply to dismiss observations involving larger, more widely followed companies would be a colossal mistake—as evidenced by the many information imbalances surrounding the $250 billion company Apple. When it comes to spotting information imbalances, it is not the size of the company that matters most but, rather, the degree to which the company, product, or societal trend behind your game-changing hypothesis falls outside the scope of Wall Street's comfort zone. Over the years, investment hypotheses involving Apple products have played a significant role in helping me grow my $20,000 Big

Money portfolio to over $2,000,000. That such gross game-changing information imbalances can repeatedly surface at one of the world's largest and most scrutinized companies can only make us wonder how many other information imbalances are waiting to be discovered.

8

YOU HAVE PEOPLE, TOO!

Monetizing Your Virtual Network

My younger brother is a "gamer" who, as a teen, rarely got out much or even saw the light of day. So, for his twenty-first birthday, I offered to take him on a weekend trip to wherever he wished. While I hoped he'd choose Vegas, I can't say I was surprised when he requested I take him to the E3 video gaming conference in downtown Los Angeles, an annual event attended by fifty thousand-plus trade professionals and droves of socially challenged computer and video gaming fans. I reluctantly agreed to his request.

To my surprise, over the course of the two-day trip I would have my eyes opened to a video game industry on the brink of an extraordinary technology-driven expansion. There was an inescapable buzz at the conference among the professional attendees in anticipation of the release of the long-awaited Sony PS3 and Microsoft Xbox 360 gaming consoles. Yet while these two industry heavyweights publicly battled each other for the affection of both die-hard gamers and the gaming press, the chatter among casual gamers and nongamers attending the conference was focused on a much less-hyped gaming console in the making by longtime industry underdog Nintendo.

Nintendo's gaming console, oddly named Wii—as in "we," to emphasize that the console is "for everyone"—used an infrared motion-sensing game controller that, while completely novel to the video game industry, happened to be grossly underpowered in terms of its ability to render rich graphics when compared with the new consoles being touted by Sony and Microsoft. For this reason, few if any serious video gamers, members of the video game press, or analysts on Wall Street who followed the video game industry paid much attention to Nintendo or its (then considered) "gimmicky" Wii console. The mere notion that an underpowered console, designed by an industry-lagging video game company that had been playing catch-up to Microsoft and Sony for nearly two decades, would emerge as an industry game-changing device was laughable.

Yet just as with iPhone, which provided a window into the future of mobile computing, and *Avatar*, which was seen as the future of filmed entertainment, a mere five minutes playing the Wii in person was all it took for me and other industry outsiders not biased by Sony's and Microsoft's perceived industry dominance to see the future of video gaming.

To the surprise of the video game industry and those who get paid to forecast gaming trends on Wall Street, Nintendo went against all odds to sell more Wii consoles during its launch year than Sony PS3s and Microsoft Xbox 360s combined, eventually selling more than seventy million units worldwide and breaking the record for most video game consoles sold in a single month. In the two-year period following Wii's launch, the price of Nintendo's publicly traded stock, which at one point comprised nearly my entire Big Money portfolio, would soar from under $15 to over $70.

My younger brother's deep insight and interest in the world of video games paved the way for me to discover game-changing information that would pay for the cost of his birthday trip a hundredfold. Over the years, the wide array of people in my life, my video-game-obsessed brother included, have broadened my range of vision related to information discovery in ways I would have never imagined possible.

MONETIZING YOUR NETWORK

In chapter 4 we discussed using the 100× multiplier effect on OPM (Other People's Money) to find a new way of thinking that could motivate us to change our behaviors. For example, anyone of us could easily save $10 by making simple changes in our spending patterns, such as going to the half-price matinee or skipping the overpriced movie popcorn. But we also considered the possibility that the $10 savings by itself might not be enough of an incentive to motivate some of us to change entrenched behaviors.

However, we also witnessed how a simple mental calculation has the potential to change our motivation. Just take the $10 savings and multiply it by a hundred. With the magic of basic arithmetic, our motivation is now $1,000. And that might be enough to get us to pass on the popcorn. (Remember, OPM is money we will use for funding our Big Money account. Our working assumption is that, over a defined period of time, whatever contribution we make to our Big Money account has the potential to increase in value by a factor of one hundred, when invested aggressively to chase game-changing information.)

For most of us, $1,000 has a greater motivational value than $10.

With the newly discovered profit potential in mind, we look at the same tub of popcorn in a whole different light. It's not simply about calories saved, but about the potential profit to be made from redeploying the savings into our Big Money account for aggressive investment in the stock market. (Remember, because our Big Money account is funded with OPM, it's money we're not afraid to lose. So we can allow ourselves to take bigger risks with it.)

What if I told you that you could also take the observational power of your "investor's glasses" and multiply this by one hundred? Would it then be reasonable to conclude that you could multiply your chances of finding game-changing information by a similar factor?

Every person crossing your path during the course of your daily life—family, neighbors, friends, coworkers, the UPS driver, hairdresser, electrician, pool boy, physician, veterinarian, pharmacist, and even the Starbucks barista—has the potential to help you widen your range of observation and your chances of discovering game-changing information. Beyond those in close physical proximity, you can use the power of the Internet and its many search engines and social networks to dramatically expand the size and scope of your "virtual network." It's an expansive universe, buzzing with information that's only a mouse click away. In the process of exploring it, you will tap into an almost limitless source of potentially game-changing information, sending you well on the road to the discovery of untold investment opportunities. Thanks to the ambition and creativity of a global army of whiz kid technology programmers from Silicon Valley to Bangalore, India, information gathering—even of the game-changing variety—has never been easier.

FINDING INFORMATION
Needles in a Global Haystack

For better or worse, we live in a world largely defined by instant gratification. If you are anything like the rest of us, caught up in the hustle and bustle of modern life, with its e-tickets, express checkouts, and on-demand programming, you expect things to happen on your time. You don't expect to wait.

Need a recipe for leek soup for tonight's dinner party? You know exactly where to go and what to do. It's second nature, really. Just hop on your trusty, all-purpose search engine and enter the appropriate keywords. In the blink of an eye, you've tapped into the shared mind-set of millions to get information you can use right now.

You can take control of your quest for game-changing information in the same way and with the same sense of urgency—with the understanding that, by the time such information is served up on a silver platter by the mass media, it has by definition already reached "information parity."

If the World Wide Web can deliver up recipes for leek soup on demand, the question you should be asking yourself right now is "How can I use all this online technology to increase my exposure to game-changing information?"

One answer is Facebook.

January 18, 2010
ALEXIS MCCAIN Oh my! Chuggington?!!! I think my kids have died and gone to heaven! I'm pretty sure this is the greatest thing that has ever happened in their lifetime . . .
2 hours ago · Comment · Like

KARIN GILBERT Um . . . and it is . . . ???
about an hour ago

ALEXIS MCCAIN new choo-choo train show on disney channel. it premiered yesterday and we've watched the first episode
about 9 times . . .
about an hour ago

COURTNEY ANDREWS My son saw it too this morning. I was
on the computer and thought to myself he is being way too
quiet. Walked in the living room and he was glued to the tv.
24 minutes ago

Alexis McCain, parent of five-year-old twin boys, is a close family
friend and happens to be a member of my social network on Facebook. I do not know Karin Gilbert or Courtney Andrews, other than
that they are both members of Alexis's Facebook network. Their comments were posted along with those of Alexis on my Facebook news-
feed that January morning.

Within days of reading the *Chuggington* observation on Facebook,
I had completed my investigative due diligence (even using Facebook
to question other moms), proven true a game-changing hypothesis
not yet widely recognized by Wall Street, and made an information arbitrage investment in Ludorum, an eleven-employee British
television production company and creator of the emerging hit show
Chuggington.

Not surprising, word of mouth helped spur on the show's popularity in North America, and within months Ludorum's stock price
would go on to climb by nearly 50 percent.

As evidenced by the chance discovery of *Chuggington* on Facebook, social and professional networks of the likes of Facebook, LinkedIn, and Twitter can be leveraged as online resources to further expand your "virtual network" and dramatically shorten the window of time for both the discovery of game-changing information and the conducting of investigative due diligence.

INVESTOR SOCIAL NETWORKS

A transformational, if little talked about, development in the investing world has been taking place for more than fifteen years: the quiet emergence of investor social networks. Believe it or not, thanks to the early pioneering vision of engineers and developers at Yahoo!, investor social networking (even though no one at the time was using this terminology) has been around for as long, if not longer than, most of the self-proclaimed "social networks" of today: LinkedIn (a "professional network") was launched in 2003; Facebook (a "social utility"), in 2004; Twitter (a "microblogging" platform), in 2006. By comparison, investors have been sharing game-changing information on Yahoo! Finance message boards since the mid-to-late 1990s!

Indeed, almost a decade before Facebook was dreamed up in a college dorm room, Yahoo! Inc. (at the time known for its Web portal) launched Yahoo! Finance with little fanfare as its first stand-alone "niche community." In this case, the niche was self-directed investors. The term *social network* wasn't even part of the vernacular at the time. Yet, with millions of investors connecting daily via hundreds of thousands of messages posted to tens of thousands of public message boards, that's effectively what it was and, in many ways, still is today.

By force of inertia as much as anything else, Yahoo! Finance has managed to hold onto its status as the undisputed eight-hundred-pound gorilla in the room. That's not to say its preeminence hasn't been challenged. In April of 2006, Google announced the beta release of its newest product, Google Finance, in a largely unsuccessful bid to muscle into Yahoo! Finance's territory on the strength of its own immensely popular online brand. However, reception by the self-directed investor crowd was lukewarm at best.

The lesser-known story is the rise of upstart competitor InvestorVillage.com. IV, as it is affectionately called by its users, was at the right place at the right time, catching a lucky break in mid-2006 when Yahoo! Finance made an ill-informed change to the design of its message board format in a way that negatively impacted a core component of its functionality. This change drove many loyal users to seek refuge in more hospitable surroundings. InvestorVillage attracts hundreds of thousands of self-directed investors each month versus the millions of users enjoyed by Yahoo! Finance. Yet the quality, diversity, and sharing nature of the investors on InvestorVillage make it my hands-down favorite among the investor social networking sites.

While largely anonymous message board users can claim to be whatever they want (let's say a "patent attorney"), it's the back-and-forth on the board that culls the wheat from the chaff and reveals a fraud from the real deal—something that is easier to do inside smaller communities such as InvestorVillage. Having posted at InvestorVillage.com for several years, and having met, either virtually or in person, with other site users, I can attest to the quality and transparency of the information being shared among many of the people—be they the attorneys, physicians, accountants, scientists, farmers, or oil field workers—who use IV's stock boards every day.

Stock message-board sites have opened up entirely new avenues for the dissemination and sharing of market-related information among self-directed investors around the world, in real time, and in a way never before possible.

April 5, 2009

I learn of a friend who has recently been diagnosed with melanoma (skin cancer). While browsing the Internet for melanoma treatment options, I stumble across a biotech company by the name of Delcath Systems. Delcath is on the verge of completing FDA clinical trials for a novel, minimally invasive procedure to treat melanoma-induced liver cancer by employing highly concentrated doses of ultra-targeted chemotherapy.

Using catheter balloons to isolate the patient's liver chamber, the procedure allows for these doses of chemotherapy—ten times what the human body can normally withstand—to be injected directly into the sealed liver chamber. The toxic, chemo-infused blood is then manually extracted out of the sealed liver chamber, cleaned using a carbon filtration machine, and returned to the body nearly chemo-free, via a return catheter placed in the patient's neck. More chemotherapy where you want it, less where you don't.

Should Delcath receive FDA approval upon completion of clinical trials, the small biotech company would be able to sell hundreds of millions to billions of dollars of its procedural targeted-chemotherapy catheter kits worldwide.

This small nine-employee biotech company is completely off Wall Street's radar. No established investment firm provides analysis coverage on the company, nor do any mutual funds or institutions of size own shares of the company's stock. After many hours scouring the Internet for more information about the company I come across a group of several dozen self-directed Delcath investors sharing information on an InvestorVillage message board.

April 6, 2009

While browsing through months of old messages on Delcath's stock message board on InvestorVillage, I am flabbergasted after reading what several of the board's active members working in unison have been able to uncover as a result of their extensive Internet data-mining efforts. The InvestorVillage members located and collected game-changing clinical trial data on seven of the ninety-two patients enrolled in Delcath's phase-three FDA clinical trial. Several of the "found" patients had massive liver tumors that had gone into remission or completely disappeared.

The message board users found this obscure patient information in local hometown newspaper articles and in TV network interviews. Since Delcath was not specifically mentioned by name in the local news reports, the stories were not publicly linked to national news-wires or easily accessible to the company's investors or the biotech analysts on Wall Street. Even more insightful were the melanoma medical forum posts and blog posts of Delcath trial patients, who had been formally documenting online, in near real time, the progress of their Delcath targeted-chemotherapy treatments.

One patient even went so far as to have her husband upload a video diary of her treatments and recovery status daily to YouTube. One of her videos captured footage of her physician revealing to her and her husband that all of the hospital's patients who were participating in the trial had experienced successful tumor remission. All seven of the "found" patients participating in Delcath's clinical trial were showing signs of clear, if not miraculous, tumor remission.

April 20, 2009

I purchase Delcath's publicly traded stock at a per-share price of $2.73.

April 21, 2010 (one year later)

Delcath publicly announces that its phase-three clinical trial has successfully met the study's primary endpoint in patients with melanoma metastases to the liver. "With the treatment arm having a median hPFS (progression-free survival) of more than three-fold that of the control arm, we easily exceeded our expectations of clinical trial success," says Eamonn P. Hobbs, president and CEO of Delcath.

The trial data point to the strong likelihood that Delcath's treatment will receive FDA approval. Patients suffering from melanoma-induced cancer of the liver who have very few viable options for survival have reason to celebrate—along with investors in Delcath, who now include both Fidelity Investments and the Blackstone Group (two of the world's largest financial companies), as users of InvestorVillage's Delcath message board watch the company's share price rise to an all-time high of $12.93—nearly five times what it traded at just one year prior.

Most clinical trials include a treatment group (those who receive the experimental treatment) and a control group (those who do not receive the experimental treatment). In pharmaceutical clinical trials, the treated patient receives the active drug, and the control group patient unknowingly receives a placebo pill. Information related to the treatment and control groups is confidential, unknown even to the doctor administering the treatment. This is referred to in the biotech industry as a "double-blind" trial, since both patient and doctor are blind to the patient's trial status. This type of study is standard protocol in nearly all FDA clinical trials.

I typically avoid making investments in biotech companies involved in this type of trial—often referred to as "lottery ticket" investments—since it is nearly impossible for me to find an information imbalance and gain an information advantage over Wall Street and other investors. I do, however, have an interest in biotech investments where creative investigative due diligence can provide a window of visibility into the degree of success of the company's pending FDA clinical trials.

Unlike pharmaceutical companies that manufacture drugs, medical device companies that perform physical surgery as part of their clinical trials occasionally offer such visibility, due to the inability to "blind" the control group. (Those undergoing surgery obviously know they are part of the treatment group, in the same manner that those in the trial who do not receive surgery know they are in the control group.)

As evidenced by the little known but public stories of the seven found patients in the Delcath trial, the very existence of the Internet makes it difficult to keep news of a life-saving surgical procedure quiet—even more so when that procedure involves a life-extending treatment for cancer. One can only wonder how many other patients in clinical trials around the world are posting updates on their personal blogs, Facebook, and YouTube and sharing the information with other patients in online support groups or through local hometown newspapers and television news.

Remarkably, the revolutionary trend in investor communication via investor social networking sites such as InvestorVillage has taken place just below the radar of millions of retail and professional investors. This phenomenon can be explained in large part by the unique demographic of the investing world. People with enough money in the market to take investing seriously tend to be older, many in their forties, fifties, sixties, and beyond. This demographic is noticeably more technologically challenged and less computer and Web savvy than younger people (who, though more aware of social networking trends online, do not yet perceive themselves as having discretionary income to put aside for speculating in the stock market).

If you are surprised to see me refer to stock message boards as "investor social networks," don't be. After all, people who frequent such sites share a common interest in their investments. And because the information flowing on the boards concerns fluctuations of the money they have at risk, many of these people follow the boards very closely, reading every message posted, hoping to get a jump on the broader pool of professional stock market participants should another member of the community uncover game-changing information.

PANNING FOR GOLD IN THE "NEW" WILD WEST

In 1848 (when the telegraph was the closest thing to tweeting that anyone could imagine) a local merchant named Sam Brannan made his way through the streets of San Francisco boldly proclaiming that there was gold in the nearby American River. Brannan's words inspired a generation of ambitious risk takers to pursue their dreams of striking it rich.

While the dreams themselves may have seemed glamorous at the time (and may even seem glamorous to us today), the reality of gold prospecting was anything but. For many folks, seeking their fortunes required traveling long distances across inhospitable lands. And panning for gold on the banks of rivers was tedious work from sunup to sundown.

But the hard work *could* pay off big. That's what kept the miners coming back. After all, the gold was there to be found, and the smart-est prospectors knew what to look for and how to find it. Many highly active stock message boards are potential gold mines of game-changing information there for the taking. But sorting out the valu-able information from fool's gold likewise requires smarts, tenacity, and powers of observation.

If you've visited popular stock message boards only casually (per-haps by accident, possibly because an investor friend once suggested that you do, or maybe you took a break from reading this book to check them out), you might have been turned off by all the dirt and muck you found the first time you dipped your virtual pan into the fast and furious flow of the informational river.

Based on this unfortunate experience, it's likely you assumed that only "foul-mouthed, adrenaline junkie day-trader" types used these boards and that there was little of value in them for you. Or you might have thought that spending a few minutes every day on a mes-sage board wasn't really worth it. Why bother? You're smart. You can do your own research. You don't need to deal with all the noise—and there is plenty of noise to sift through on every board.

But when used as one of the many weapons in an information-gathering and investigative due diligence arsenal, investor social net-works represent an extraordinary accumulation of brainpower, and it would be foolish not to tap into it. The primary thing that a stock message board service and its collective brain power can do for you is give you a timing advantage. And not only do you have access to game-changing information before other investors do (hence the "early bird" timing advantage), but you also have access to five, ten, or even a hundred times as many pieces of game-changing informa-tion as you would on your own. Add it all up and it's really staggering what you could achieve with that sort of head start.

The old adage goes "Two heads are better than one," and stock message boards give you access to hundreds and even thousands of heads. And believe me, you will find this many, if not more, active message-board posters on popular stock messages boards on any given trading day. It's up to you to mine these boards for their vast stores of informational riches.

"COOPETITION"

In his book *The Wisdom of Crowds*, James Surowiecki explores the potential that large groups of people have for generating smarter answers to questions and better solutions to problems collectively than any one person might produce on his own.

Surowiecki also studies situations that pose unique challenges to his premise. For example, he cites paying taxes and determining appropriate wages as examples of what he calls "cooperation problems," which he defines as "problems involv[ing] the challenge of getting self-interested, distrustful people to work together, even when narrow self-interest would seem to dictate that no individual should take part."[12]

To his examples I would add the challenge of trying to determine the potential upside of an investment in a given company at a specific point. Put another way, if I believe that Delcath represents a strong information arbitrage investment opportunity, why should I share my opinion on a stock message board with total strangers who could then easily compete with (i.e. bid against) me for those same shares, increasing their cost?

Well, believe it or not, there are many reasons why this might not be as irrational an act as it might seem at first blush. For example, even though you think you are correct, you might want to see if other investors agree with you—much like seeking a second opinion for a medical condition. If they don't, perhaps they will push you to do better due diligence and make a smarter decision for yourself.

Or you might see some karmic value in sharing your research and opinions with other investors. If you share your painstaking research and help someone else make money, it's not unreasonable to assume they might wish to share their best information discovery and due diligence with you, too, in the hopes of fostering a profitable long-term collaboration.

Then there's the time value: that is, the ability to get information faster than the broader market, thanks to the efficiencies of online collaboration. If you think you can keep up with news quickly because you have a Google alert set for your favorite stock, or your online broker streams you real-time news from just-released press releases from the company you are following, imagine if you had dozens (to say nothing of hundreds) of people in different disciplines scouring the Web day and night for information. With so many sources of potential information flowing through the funnel of the message board, you're now plugged into many more heads than your own, and you can tap into the discerning power of human observation and interpretation in a way that even Google can't fully harness or even approximate.

Of course, if you've already purchased all the shares you want, then you have little to lose from the competition. By the same token, you have something to gain if a message board user who disagrees with you challenges you and helps you uncover potentially detrimental game-changing information you otherwise would have missed on your own. This sense of cooperation toward the achievement of a common goal among people who would ordinarily view themselves to be in competition with one another is known as coopetition.

I'm not saying that you should accept out of hand what the crowd proclaims or believes to be true. I'm saying you should use the crowd as a tool of discovery—to poke and prod and stir things up. Use other people online to help you discover new information. And keep your eyes and mind open to new possibilities.

FROM CHOOSING MOTOR OIL TO PICKING STOCKS
The Wisdom of Crowds Examined

Because I live in a three-story urban town house, I'm no lawn-care expert. While helping my parents out by mowing their lawn early one Saturday morning, I noticed their mower running hot and decided to check the oil (something I had the uneasy suspicion they had not done in quite some time). While it wasn't bone dry, it was clearly low, even to an untrained eye like mine.

The only motor oil I could find in their garage was a quart of Castrol Syntec 5W-40 SAE for their car, but I wasn't sure if I could use it in their Briggs & Stratton–powered lawn mower. Now, I could have just poured some in and hoped for the best. And honestly, that would have been my solution fifteen years ago. But now that a quick online search makes it so easy to do just about any type of due diligence, it made more sense to start there.

After clicking through a few of the top results for "5W-40 lawn mower," I found a blog that had over a dozen answers. I didn't consciously think, "Hey, I'm going to tap into the wisdom of crowds." It just sort of came with the territory, I suppose. It's something we take for granted online. To quote Surowiecki again, "under the right circumstances, groups are remarkably intelligent, and are often smarter than the smartest people in them."[13]

The bloggers' answers all seemed articulate and relevant. More important, they seemed to be in agreement with one another. Almost every one of them recommended using 5W-30 or at least a 30-weight motor oil. (I still don't know what the weight means exactly; all I knew was that it was better to be safe than sorry.) So I ran out and picked up a quart of 5W-30. If no one online was recommending 40-weight, that was good enough for me.

You can leverage the wisdom of the crowd on a stock message board to similar effect. With a little effort, you might find someone—whether a neighbor, a friend on Facebook, or a stock message board user—willing and able to provide you with valuable information in its purest form: that is, specialized information or knowledge not commonly shared. Perhaps this person is a beverage distributor and can help you uncover the next hot trend in energy/health drinks. Maybe he's a physician who can help you decipher a scientific abstract discussing the benefits of some new therapeutic drug you've stumbled across and are considering investing in. This information might be directly relevant to a stock you're considering buying or have already invested in. By cooperating with other minds, particularly when they bring to the table expertise you don't possess, you can reap an informational advantage.

Sometimes those other minds provide an added bonus: information about new or collapsing trends you might not even be aware of yet but are well positioned to understand and take advantage of. It's not knowing what to do with the information that's hindering you. It's there being only one of you. But in a social network of people seeking out and sharing game-changing information, all of sudden you can multiply yourself, or at least your own curiosity and hard work, many times over.

Let's say you're an ice-cream-aholic. Every Saturday morning you run to the frozen food section of your local grocery store and load a gallon tub of Chocolate-Chocolate Heaven into your cart. You regularly exchange information pertaining to newly launched ice-cream flavors with like-minded ice-cream aficionados across the Internet. The only problem is there's nothing "game changing" going on with ice cream in your own neighborhood. On the other side of the country, however, someone else resides in a test market for a soon-to-be-launched fat-burning, negative-calorie concept that is the future of ice cream. If that person shares this information with you in person, on Facebook, or on an investing message board, now it's something to which you can apply your skills.

Or let's say you are curious about trends in apparel for toddlers. With only one child, your experience is limited. But what if you were able to go online and get opinions from dozens or even hundreds of other parents. Now you have the ability to identify and validate trends by using the multiplier effect. Figure out how to trade your knowledge, skills, and experience with other investors in exchange for their knowledge, skills, and experience—until you have your hands on so much game-changing information that you are in a position to change your financial life through better, smarter investing.

Just be aware that for all its potential benefits, group think can cloud collective judgment. Sometimes members of a group get a false sense of "security in numbers." They run the risk of reinforcing one another's opinion because individuals don't want to be seen sticking their necks out or going against conventional wisdom—a phenomenon witnessed routinely on Wall Street. To avoid falling into this trap, always make sure to screen the opinions and background of message board users offering their opinions. View their message history. Does a particular user seem biased or do his past messages reflect a balanced view of the stock? Most important, be sure to use message board information only as a supplement to the research and due diligence you perform on your own without influence from others.

If you are a trusting person by nature, you will need to teach yourself to be skeptical. Never put yourself or your money at risk by blindly accepting information from an anonymous message board user. Make every effort to independently verify any and all claims made online, regardless of the source. You owe it to yourself and your portfolio.

Now that you have a handle on the basic history of stock message boards as investor social networks, along with a firm grasp on the underlying conceptual framework of who uses these boards and why, it's time to take a closer look under the hood at the actual mechanics of using such services in a way that maximizes your ability to find and profit from the game-changing information they contain.

9

FAKE IT TILL YOU MAKE IT!

How Stock Options Can "Super-Size" Your Investment Returns

"Remember the turtle—he never makes any
progress till he sticks his neck out."
—UNKNOWN

While pursuing investment possibilities, you stumble across a promising information arbitrage opportunity involving the stock of an emerging youth apparel company frequented by your teenage daughter and nearly every one of her friends. Your due diligence validates a game-changing investment hypothesis that is not yet widely known or accepted as fact by Wall Street. For the first time it appears that your daughter's fixation with fashion and shopping could positively impact your family's finances.

Thanks to a few painless cost-cutting measures such as washing your own car, mowing your own yard, and switching from name-brand to store-brand groceries, you have been able to contribute $3,000 of OPM to your Big Money investing account. A great start, but far from the $500,000 you have determined you will need to quit your job and enter early retirement. In the event that your game-changing investment hypothesis turns out to be correct, it is important that you get the biggest bang for your investment buck. So what's next?

Up until this point we have learned that the path to investment success requires you to:

1. Create a Big Money account.
2. Apply the 100× money multiplier effect to reveal new sources of OPM for the purpose of funding your Big Money account.
3. Unleash the observational power of your "investor's glasses" in pursuit of game-changing information.
4. Leverage the power of your personal network and the Internet to expand the size and scope of your real and virtual network.
5. Abide by the scientific method to construct, test, and validate your investment hypotheses without influence from so-called "experts" on Wall Street or in the financial media.
6. Calculate a consensus score to quantify the level of consensus or uncertainty that exists on Wall Street surrounding your game-changing investment hypothesis.

We also learned that one of the primary differences between a successful person and a failure is often the courage to bet on one's ideas, to take calculated risks, and to act. The intended purpose of having a designated Big Money account funded with Other People's Money is to empower you to do exactly that: take calculated risks on uncertain outcomes in pursuit of a potentially life-changing financial benefit—and to do so in a way that does not jeopardize the financial well-being of either you or your family.

Now that your daughter has tipped you off to what you believe to be a game-changing information imbalance in youth apparel retailing, you must decide between two very different investment paths.

PATH 1 (BUYING STOCK)

These days, buying shares of stock in a public company is nearly as straightforward as buying a gallon of milk—the one key difference being that stock prices are constantly in flux. But before you can proceed with the purchase of shares of stock in a company, you must first determine how many shares you can afford to buy. If a single share is trading for $10, then your $3,000 could buy you three hundred shares. At a price of $100 per share, you could buy thirty shares. At a price of $1,000 per share, your $3,000 buys you three shares.

Contrary to popular belief, a company that costs $100 per share, or even $1,000 per share, is not necessarily larger or more "expensive" than a company with a share price of $10. If a company were a pizza, a share of its stock would be equivalent to a single slice of pizza. Say you have two pizzas of identical size, pizza A and pizza B. You slice pizza A up into four really fat slices and B into thirty-two really skinny slices. You decide to charge $2 for a slice of pizza A and $1 for a slice of pizza B. In this scenario, pizza A (at $2 per slice) is actually priced much cheaper than pizza B (at $1 per slice), as a person would have to buy eight skinny slices of pizza B (at a cost of $8) to get the same amount of pizza in a single fat $2 slice of pizza A.

Just as a pizzeria can arbitrarily determine the number of slices in each pizza, a company is able to arbitrarily determine the number of shares of its company to offer for sale in the public stock market. When priced by the slice, the only way to determine the total value or price for each whole pizza sold is to multiply the cost per slice by the total number of slices in the pizza. The same principle applies to valuing a company. A company that has divided itself into a billion shares of stock that are trading at only $3 per share is actually a very large $3 billion company, whereas a company that has divided itself into only one hundred thousand shares of stock that are trading at a much larger $30 per share would represent a relatively small $3 million company.

Stock prices and company valuations are of zero importance to information arbitrage investors, yet having a basic understanding of what owning a share of stock in a company represents is helpful if for nothing more than improving your ability to converse intelligently with other self-directed investors.

If a single share of the Emerging Youth Apparel Company you want to invest in (hypothetical stock symbol EYAC) were trading for $10, you could afford to buy three hundred shares with the $3,000 in your Big Money account (not including brokerage commissions, which range between $7 and $15 per trade for online brokers).

So how much ownership in the company does your three hundred shares represent? Figuring out your total ownership is an easy, fun exercise that will provide you with tremendous perspective on what you are actually purchasing each time you buy stock in a company.

To do this, simply find out how many shares of stock the prospective company has divided itself into by searching the "shares outstand-ing" field of the Key Statistics section of your stock's quotes page on Yahoo! Finance (finance.yahoo.com). To determine your percentage of ownership in the company, divide the number of shares outstand-ing by the number of shares you either own or are seeking to pur-chase. If the entire Emerging Youth Apparel Company were divided up into three thousand total shares of stock, your three-hundred-share purchase would mean that you now owned 10 percent of the company (300/3,000). That means that 10 percent of the company's profits belong to you. If the company were to distribute 100 percent of its profits via dividend payments to shareholders (which they rarely do), you would receive a check for 10 percent of the company's profits every year, no different than if you owned 10 percent of a local pizzeria. Of course, it's more realistic that the company would be di-vided into something like *thirty million* shares, meaning that your three-hundred-share purchase would give you ownership of just one one thousandth of 1 percent of the company.

Now that you understand what it is you're buying, physically pur-chasing the shares of a publicly traded company will require that you either phone or visit in person your broker's branch office, or log on to your online broker's Web site. But before you do this, you will need to be prepared to make a few decisions related to the act of pur-chasing or selling stock.

Order Type: Whether to Place a "Market" or a "Limit" Order

Every publicly traded stock has a "bid" and an "ask" price that fluc-tuate based on supply and demand, from the opening of the market to the close of the market (9:30 AM–4:00 PM EST). Much like at an auction, the current bid price for a company's stock represents the highest price someone is willing to pay for shares at that moment in time. The current ask price represents the lowest price that someone is asking for (i.e., looking to sell their shares for) at that moment in time. The bid and ask prices often change second by second, thousands of times each day.

When placing a "market order," you are agreeing to buy shares of stock at the going market ask price, or to sell shares of stock at the going market bid price. If you were to ask a friend to buy a gallon of milk, you would be placing a "market" order for that milk, as it is unlikely that you would place a "limit" on how much you were willing to reimburse your friend for purchasing the milk on your behalf. You provide him with the flexibility to pay whatever the going price is at the grocery store. The market determines what you should pay for the milk.

Why are you willing to do this? Because the convenience of not having to ask your friend to price-shop the city for an inexpensive, perishable product such as milk outweighs the financial risk of the grocery store suddenly deciding to charge an unreasonable price for the milk. (Plus, it increases the likelihood that your friend will be willing to do you another favor at some point in the future.) When you have lots of buyers and sellers for a particular item, such as milk, the forces of supply and demand result in an efficient market of fair pricing for everyone involved. This is a good thing.

The stock market's closest equivalent to buying a gallon of milk would be buying one hundred shares of an actively traded stock such as Apple or Google. As I write this sentence, the current bid for Apple stock is $258.26, and the current ask for Apple stock is $258.35. If I were to place a market order to buy one hundred shares of Apple stock, I would be sold those shares at the current, lowest ask price of $258.35, just pennies more than the highest bid price ($258.26) I could instantly resell those shares in the open market. The large number of buyers and sellers for large, popular stocks such as Apple makes for an efficient, highly liquid, and fair market where it is generally safe and prudent to place market orders to buy and sell stock—no different than you would do for a gallon of milk.

Now, suppose you were to ask that same friend to attend an art auction and bid on a one-of-a-kind painting on your behalf. In this case, you would likely want to set a ceiling, or maximum price you are willing to pay for the painting. Art auctions can be volatile, and the combination of eccentric bidders and unique merchandise can occasionally lead people to bid up items beyond their fair value. (This doesn't even account for the presence of planted "shills," bidders who have been known to artificially drive up auction prices with phony bids.)

In a contrasting scenario, if you were to sell a painting at a local auction with a limited number of bidders, you would be wise to put a floor (or minimum price) you were willing to accept for your painting. This would ensure that the lack of a robust market for your painting did not result in an unjustly low selling price.

A "limit" order is one in which a price ceiling or price floor is used to buy or sell stock. Unfortunately, not all stocks have a market of buyers and sellers as extensive as Apple or Google. When an investor decides to buy or sell a large number of shares in a company that is small and not actively traded, the balance of supply and demand can become temporarily disrupted, causing a sudden, self-induced rise or drop in the price of the stock. For example, if you place an order to buy five thousand shares of stock X, and that happens to be half of the total available shares of stock X being offered on the market that particular day, a market order might only get you your first one thousand shares at the price you expect. The very act of your buying the share will elevate the demand and the share price, so your next one thousand shares will be more expensive, and your next one thousand even more expensive. In this situation, it is wise for the investor to place a limit order with his broker to buy the stock at a predetermined maximum price usually no higher than the current asking price, or to sell the stock at a minimum predetermined price usually no less than the current bid price.

In the event that your limit order does not result in the intended purchase or sale of stock—or results in only a partial purchase or sale—you can raise or lower your limit order price until your buy/sell order is completely filled. This penny pinching cat-and-mouse game between those seeking to buy stock at the lowest possible price and those seeking to sell stock at the highest possible price has the potential to add drama and a bit of frustration for self-directed investors seeking a no-hassle transaction.

For most stock transactions, most of the time the convenience of placing a market order far outweighs the risk that the order will cause you to overpay or undersell. The time to consider using a limit order is when buying or selling a relatively large number of shares in a relatively small or sparsely traded company whose stock does not have a large, active market of buyers and sellers.

How will you know when this is the case? Here's a rule of thumb I use: if the number of shares you are planning to buy or sell, when multiplied by one thousand, equals a number that is larger than your stock's "average daily trading volume" (listed on your stock's Yahoo! Finance quote page as AvgVol), you might consider placing a limit order. I also tend to place limit orders for any total stock purchase exceeding $25,000. Until you are comfortable with the process of placing limit orders, I suggest you do so with guidance from a representative at your online broker. The mission of all discount and online brokers is to assist and educate newbie investors so that they become proficient self-directed investors. Your customer service rep should be happy to assist.

Duration: Whether to Place a "Day" or "Until Cancel" Order

In the world of real estate, a formal offer to purchase a home is nearly always accompanied by a specified period of time, in hours or days, in which the homeowner has to accept the offer. If the owner does not accept the offer within the defined period of time set by the buyer, the offer expires.

In the context of buying and selling stocks, a "day/today" order, if not executed (i.e., completed) by the broker or canceled by the customer by the 4:00 PM EST close of market on the day it is placed, expires automatically. A "good until cancel" or "open" order remains in effect until it is either executed by the broker or canceled by the customer.

Since nearly all market orders, and even most limit orders, to buy and sell stock at the going market price are instantaneously executed by your broker, the only time any of this comes into play is when you attempt to use limit orders to buy stock at a price lower than the current market ask price, or to sell stock at a price higher than the current market bid price. This is no different from when someone makes a below-market, "low-ball" offer for a house.

As information arbitrage investors who are not attempting to trade in and out of stocks multiple times a day or seeking to profit from tiny fluctuations in the price of stock, we do not concern ourselves with such pricing games, and therefore have no reason to place anything other than what is considered to be the default "day" order. In nearly twenty years of investing, fat finger mistakes aside, I have yet to place anything other than "day" orders to buy or sell stock.

Let's review the steps you would take to purchase $3,000 of stock in the hypothetical Emerging Youth Apparel Company:

1. Enter the company name "Emerging Youth Apparel Company" into the Get Quotes field on Yahoo! Finance (or a similar field on your online broker's Web site) to retrieve the company's stock symbol EYAC, in addition to the current market ask price of $10.00 per share.

2. Not including broker commissions (usually $7–$15 per transaction), divide the total amount of money you want to invest in EYAC ($3,000) by the current per-share market ask price ($10) to determine the number of shares you can afford to purchase ($3,000/$10 = 300 shares).

3. If the number of shares you intend to purchase (three hundred), when multiplied by one thousand, equals a number that is larger than EYAC's average daily trading volume as listed in the AvgVol field on EYAC's Yahoo! Finance quote page, you might consider placing a limit order under the guidance of a representative at your online broker. This scenario is unlikely, unless you are investing either a large amount of money or in an extremely small company.

4. To place a market order, call or visit a branch office, or log on to your online broker's Web site to place "a *market* order good for *today* to *purchase* three hundred shares of stock

symbol EYAC." When the time comes to sell your shares, you will simply place "a *market* order good for *today* to *sell* three hundred shares of stock symbol EYAC."

5. To place a limit order, call or visit your broker's branch office, or log on to the broker's Web site to place "a *limit* order good for *today* to *purchase* three hundred shares of stock symbol EYAC at a limit price of $10 per share." When the time comes to sell your shares, you will simply place "a *limit* order good for *today* to *sell* three hundred shares of stock symbol EYAC at a limit price of (*insert current bid price*) per share." Remember, limit orders to buy stock should usually be entered at the current ask price, while limit orders to sell stock should usually be entered at the current bid price.

6. Confirm over the phone, in person, or by logging onto your online brokerage account that your order to buy the stock was indeed executed and that you are now the owner of three hundred shares of the Emerging Youth Apparel Company.

Unless you are lactose intolerant, it does not really benefit you to know anything about lactose-free milk. The same thing applies to investing terms. In the event that you come across foreign investment terms you don't understand—such as *stop limit, trailing stop,* or *all or none*—don't be alarmed. These terms, along with hundreds of others, were left out of this book by design. They are used by sophisticated investors pursuing more complex (often needlessly so) investment transactions that you, as an information arbitrage investor, have zero need to understand.

Do you recall, as a child, asking your teacher or parents why you had to learn algebra if you had no intention of using it in real life? If so, you likely received an answer along the lines of brain development, college preparation, or, as in my case, "because I said so." Now that you're a self-sustaining adult with a fully mature brain, chances are these answers likely no longer apply to you. As such, there isn't a need to fill your head with mind-numbing, useless financial gibberish that is neither interesting nor relevant to your becoming a successful information arbitrage investor.

Now that you understand the basic principles of how to find, validate, and act on investment opportunities, what else could there possibly be left to learn? Let me answer that question with another question. As an information arbitrage investor, is it possible to turn a few thousand dollars into a million dollars or more by simply buying the stock of the "right" three or four companies over the course of a few years?

The answer is yes! As proven by the Ugg/True Religion/Crocs example, it is absolutely possible. But that doesn't mean it isn't extraordinarily difficult or that, in practice, you are likely ever to do so. Sure, you could earn one hundred times your money simply by making two consecutive investments that each go up by a factor of ten (first turning $1 into $10, and then turning that $10 into $100). The problem is that even among the most lucrative information arbitrage investments, a tenfold rise in value over a short period of time, while possible, is the exception and not the rule. While that sort of dramatic rise may happen from time to time, an increase in stock price ranging from 30 percent to 300 percent from the point of information imbalance (when you buy) to the point of information parity (when you sell) is more realistic.

When charting out your future riches, you would be wise to anticipate a winning percentage that is somewhat less than perfect. This will further slow your timeline for turning $1 into $100. If you were to pursue four information arbitrage investments over a five-year period, expect one of those four investments to flop—either due to an oversight in your due diligence or through no fault of your own. Sometimes overriding forces, such as geopolitical terrorism or a global economic credit crisis, can cause the value of the stock market (and your investment) to fluctuate. These are reasons you could never have anticipated or controlled.

So if you are content to *slowly* build a *small* fortune for yourself, perhaps doubling the value of your Big Money investment account every one to two years (not that there's anything wrong with that), feel free to stop reading this chapter now. You already have all the tools you need to monetize your game-changing investment observations and hypotheses. But if your objective is to *quickly* build a *large* fortune for yourself, much in the way I turned $20,000 into over $2 million in a three-year period, you will need to learn how to super-size your investment dollars while applying the magical tools of leverage I first learned as a teenager.

PATH 2 (WOULD YOU LIKE TO SUPER-SIZE THAT INVESTMENT?)

Let's put stock investing aside for a moment. Say one morning, while discussing the previous night's *American Idol* performances with coworkers over the office water cooler, you come across a juicy tidbit of game-changing real estate information. While volunteering at a community graffiti-removal project in a particularly neglected section of the city, a nephew of your coworker had a chance encounter with the well-known owner of the city's Major League Baseball team. The Major League franchise owner was being escorted through the streets by an entourage of city officials and land surveyors. The nephew overheard them discussing the area as the location for the baseball team's "not yet publicly announced" soon-to-be-constructed billion-dollar stadium and adjoining retail and restaurant development. The nephew observed the group pointing to a row of abandoned houses sitting atop a nearby bluff that, according to their words, "will have a direct sightline into the new baseball stadium." They jokingly referred to the dilapidated property as the "least expensive and best seats in the house!"

You and your coworkers figure that if you move quickly, before this information becomes public, you could each snatch up one of the uninhabited hillside houses for land value alone, which would cost at most $50,000. In a few months, when word of the stadium and development project location became public and buzz of the bluff's extraordinary infield views circulated among real estate investors, the value of those lots should easily double in value to $100,000. Not a bad short-term investment return!

But what if, rather than turning $50,000 into $100,000, there were a way to turn that same $50,000 into $500,000? In fact, there is. As an alternative to using your $50,000 to purchase one of the hillside properties, you could instead pay the property owner just $5,000 in exchange for an "option contract" that would give you the legal right or "option" to purchase his house at any time within the next six months at a set price of $50,000 (the fair market value of the home today).

By doing this, you are purchasing the contractual right to buy the property at a set price within a predetermined period of time, but you would in no way be obligated to purchase the property. What this means is that anytime in the next six months you have the option to buy the hillside property for $50,000. This right is guaranteed to you regardless of how much the value of the property rises between now and the expiration of your six-month option.

In the event that the baseball stadium development does not materialize, you simply walk away without purchasing the property, and lose the $5,000 previously paid to the property owner for your exclusive six-month option contract.

If the stadium development materializes as you expect, and the value of the property climbs from $50,000 to $100,000, you are in luck—because you possess an option that guarantees you the right to purchase that property at the previously set contract price of $50,000. Even better is that you do not have to purchase the property to realize your investment profit. You can instead choose to sell the option contract itself to someone else for a profit.

The option contract you paid $5,000 for would now be worth roughly $50,000 to another buyer, since that is the difference between the property's current value and the set contract price at which the holder of the option contract is legally permitted to purchase the property. In this scenario, you never took possession of the property, nor did you have to come up with the $50,000 to purchase the property. You simply sold your $5,000 option contract to another real estate investor for $50,000, ten times your initial investment.

By negotiating this same $5,000 option contract with ten different property owners, you would have turned a $50,000 investment into

$500,000, all without ever having to take ownership or pay in full for a single property. That is the magic of *leverage*.

Call Option Contracts

A call option contract provides you with the legal right, but not the obligation, to buy something at a predetermined price. Option contracts on stocks provide a way for small-time investors with limited investment dollars to control large amounts of stock for short periods of time. A typical $100 stock option investment might provide you with control over $1,000 of that company's stock for a period of a few months. Should that company's stock go on to double within that preset period, you would realize not a $100 profit but a $1,000 profit from your initial $100 stock option investment. That's ten times what you would have made had you simply purchased shares of the company's stock.

Option contracts can be leveraged by investors to either *purchase* or *sell* stock. For now we will focus on "call options," the particular type of option that provides the owner with the right (but not the obligation) to *purchase* a specific number of shares of a stock at a predetermined price and within a certain time frame. Since the set purchase price is "locked in," the value of a call option contract rises and falls in value as the price of the stock rises and falls relative to the set price at which the owner of the call contract is permitted to purchase shares of the company's stock.

There is no limit to how high an option contract can appreciate in value. The worst-case scenario for the holder of an option contract that has lost all of its value is that he will never lose more money than was paid to acquire the contract in the first place.

Call Option Contracts

When you purchase shares of stock in a company, you become a partial owner of that company, hoping to sell your shares later at a higher price. When you purchase a call option contract, most often your objective is to sell the contractual right you have acquired (to purchase shares of a company at a predetermined price) to someone else for a higher price than you paid for it. The most one can lose when purchasing an option contract is the amount of money paid to acquire the contract. Once an option contract expires, any money lost on the option contract becomes a permanent loss.

Suppose you paid $100 for a call option contract from your local gas station giving you the right (but not the obligation) to purchase up to a thousand gallons of gas anytime within the next year at a set price of $2 per gallon. Shortly after buying the contract, the market price of a gallon of gas jumps to $5. You own the right to purchase a thousand gallons of gas at a negotiated total cost of just $2,000 (1,000 × $2), instead of the $5,000 (1,000 × $5) it would cost anyone else to purchase that same amount of gas at the going rate of $5 per gallon.

Your call option contract now has $3,000 of real, "intrinsic value"—no different from a $3,000 coupon for gas. This $3,000 intrinsic value is the approximate amount the call option would be valued at in the open market were you to decide to sell it to someone else for a $2,900 profit ($3,000 sale price minus the $100 original cost of the option contract).

Now let's take a look at the opposite scenario. Shortly after purchasing the call option contract, the price of a gallon of gas at your local gas station drops from $2 to $1. In this case, the call option contract you own that gives you the right to buy gas at $2 per gallon is far from having any intrinsic value, since it would be cheaper for you simply to pay the going market rate of $1 per gallon. Consequently, the option contract's resale market value has declined and is now worth something less than the $100 you paid for it. Even so, the option contract still retains some value, referred to as "time value," since the contract does not expire for one year, and there is still plenty of time for the price of a gallon of gasoline to climb above $2, at which point the option contract will have intrinsic value.

> The going market price of a stock option contract is a combination of its real "intrinsic value" and its remaining "time value."

Learning how to invest with stock options is no different from learning how to ride a bicycle. For nearly everyone, the experience is both scary and intimidating at first, but by taking a few simple steps, anyone can learn the basics. To a good information arbitrage investor, a basic understanding of stock options can shorten the timeline for achieving financial prosperity after twenty or more years.

When compared with stock investing, stock option contracts involve a few additional moving parts. But learning to buy and sell option contracts is fundamentally no more complex than buying and selling stock in a company. As with buying stock, you will need to be prepared to make a few decisions before proceeding with your option contract purchase.

Choosing a Strike Price

We have learned that a call option contract provides the owner with the right (but not obligation) to purchase a specific number of shares of a stock at a *predetermined price* and within a certain period of time. The predetermined price is formally known as an option contract's *strike price*.

When purchasing an options contract, you may choose from any number of strike prices that might be less or greater than the company's current stock price. Strike prices are generally offered in increments of $2.50 ($10.00, $12.50, $15.00, $17.50, and so on). You can reference the Options section of a company's Yahoo! Finance quote page to view that company's entire range of available option contract strike prices.

A call option contract (the right to purchase stock) with a strike price (guaranteed purchase price) that is *greater than* the company's current stock price will be priced based purely on the call option contract's remaining time value. A call option contract with a strike price that is *less than* the company's current stock price will be priced according to the contract's intrinsic value plus any remaining time value.

Because of this intrinsic value, the lower the strike price, the more expensive the call option contract—which, if you think about it, makes perfect sense. If the going price of gas is $3 per gallon, you can appreciate how the price to own a six-month call option contract to buy gas at $1 per gallon would be more expensive than a six-month call option contract to buy gas at $5 per gallon. Who wouldn't prefer, and be willing to pay more for, the option to buy gas at $1 rather than $5?

The six-month call option contract to buy gas at $1 per gallon already has $2 of "real" intrinsic value (since the going price of gas is $3 per gallon), meaning that if you were to purchase this contract you would pay a price of at least $2, and likely more, to account for the remaining time value on the contract.

Call option contracts that have intrinsic value at the time of sale are relatively expensive to buy because they do not require a large move in stock price to appreciate in value. This type of option contract is commonly referred to as being "in the money," and is sought out by investors seeking to increase their purchasing power (known as leverage), and associated investment returns, by a factor of between two and ten.

The six-month call option contract to buy gas at $5 per gallon currently has zero intrinsic value, and would be priced based solely on the contract's remaining time value. As such, this contract would be relatively inexpensive, attracting high-risk investors who were willing to take a low-odds bet on the unlikely event that gas prices might suddenly rise above $5 per gallon before the expiration of the six-month contract period.

Option contracts that have zero intrinsic value when sold are relatively cheap to buy because they generally require big movements in stock price to become profitable for the option owner. This type of call option contract is commonly referred to as being "out of the money." Such a contract is sought out by risk-tolerant investors who are generally seeking to increase their purchasing power, and associated investment returns, by a factor of ten or greater.

A call option contract with a strike price that is *less than* the company's current stock price "in the money" already has intrinsic value, provides a small to reasonably large amount of leverage, and will expire worthless only if the stock price declines below the option strike price.

A call option contract with a strike price that is *greater than* the company's current stock price "out of the money" has zero intrinsic value, can provide an extraordinary large amount of leverage, and will expire worthless unless the stock price rises beyond that of the option contract's strike price.

As an information arbitrage investor, I get (at most) one to two opportunities over the course of any given year to pursue well-founded investments based on game-changing information imbalances. For those few investment opportunities that I do ultimately pursue, I do so with a high degree of confidence, investing between 25 percent and 50 percent of the funds in my Big Money investment portfolio. When they are available, I nearly always favor buying stock option contracts over shares of stock alone. I am willing to take on this high degree of risk in exchange for the ability to boost my investment buying power and maximize the potential return for each of my investment dollars.

This decision to take on risk is made easier by the fact that I am exclusively investing what I consider to be Other People's Money (OPM) from my Big Money investing account. Yet, even when supremely confident in predicting the directional move of a stock based on the anticipated dissemination of game-changing information, I never attempt to foretell the degree to which a stock price will move in a given period of time. There are far too many factors involved with predicting the precise increase or decrease in share price value that Wall Street or any given group of investors will place on a stock upon the dissemination of game-changing information.

Like fundamental and technical analysis, the price target game is one I have zero interest in playing. For this reason, I am usually hesitant to purchase anything but "in the money" call stock options—that is, call option contracts in which the guaranteed purchase, or "strike," price is less than the company's current stock price. When purchasing call option contracts, I generally seek out the highest available strike price that is equal to or less than the current stock price of the company in which I'm seeking to invest.

For example, assume that an $11.00 stock offers call option strike prices of $5.00, $7.50, $10.00, $12.50, and $15.00. I would purchase the option contract with the $10.00 strike price. If the stock price were $9.75, I would purchase the $7.50 strike price. Not exactly rocket science. This middle-of-the-road, measured-risk strategy usually results in my being able to increase my purchasing power by a factor of five to ten, resulting in investment returns that are five to ten times larger than if I were simply to purchase shares of the company's stock.

Choosing an Expiration Date

One last time: A call option provides the owner with the right (but not the obligation) to purchase a specific number of shares of a stock at a predetermined price and within a certain time frame. The time frame is determined by the option contract's expiration date.

With a few exceptions (such as on market holidays or when buying European-style options that expire weekly), stock option contracts expire at the closing bell of the stock market (4:00 PM EST) on the third Friday of each month. Now you know the meaning of my investing Internet alias, 3rdFriday. A January option contract would expire on the third Friday of January, and a September option contract would expire on the third Friday of September.

As a general rule, the more time remaining on an option contract, the more valuable (and costly) the contract. As time passes, and the expiration date of the contract nears, the time value portion of a contract's total value will slowly erode, until it reaches zero on the contract's expiration date.

Upon expiration, an option contract's only value, if any, lies in its intrinsic value. Time is extremely valuable to the holder of an option contract, as more time equals more opportunity for the underlying stock to make its anticipated directional move and for the contract to gain intrinsic value. For this reason it is considerably more expensive to purchase an option contract that expires in one year than one at the same strike price that expires in one month.

Going back to our hypothetical call option on gasoline, if the going rate for a gallon of gas is $3, you can appreciate how a twelve-month call option contract to buy gas at $5 per gallon would be more expensive than a one-month call option contract to buy gas at $5 per gallon. You would want (and be willing to pay extra) for additional time for the market price of a gallon of gas to rise above your $5 strike price.

Your challenge as an information arbitrage investor is to choose an expiration date that buys you enough time until Wall Street and the investing public acknowledge the validity of the game-changing information you have uncovered. Only then will your perceived information imbalance reach a point of information parity in the market—and the share price of your investment react accordingly.

For this reason, I generally purchase option contracts with expiration dates ranging from six to nine months away. Since publicly traded companies are required to announce sales and earnings every three months, the six-to-nine-month window ensures ample opportunity for the anticipated dissemination of game-changing information to the market. For event-driven information arbitrage investments—such as those involving FDA drug approvals or new product launches—it is wise to pick an expiration date that is at least one to two months beyond the anticipated event date, to account for any unexpected delays. And just because option contracts come with expiration dates does not mandate that you hold on to them through the option contract's expiration.

Just as with stock investments, any information arbitrage–based investment in an option contract should be sold (for profit or loss) immediately upon your determination that the information imbalance that served as the impetus for the investment decision has reached a point of information parity in the market. Option contracts that have positive value on their day of expiration (as defined as a bid price of $0.05 or greater) should be sold well in advance of the 4:00 PM EST market close. Otherwise, your online brokerage account will trigger a purchase of all shares represented by your option contract at the strike price—a mistake I once learned the hard way.

Once you have chosen both a strike price and an option contract expiration date, you are ready to proceed with your call option contract order. As with stock, each option contract has its very own symbol. Now that you understand the purpose of an option contract's strike price and expiration date, either decoding or constructing for yourself a stock's option contract symbol should be a breeze.

EYAC110715C10 would be the symbol for a call option contract on the Emerging Youth Apparel Company with an expiration date of July 2011 and a strike price of $10. Let's break it down:

EYAC: the symbol for the option's underlying stock, Emerging Youth Apparel Company
11: the year in which the option expires (i.e., 2011)
07: the month in which the option expires (i.e., July)
15: the exact day of the month on which the option expires (i.e., the third Friday of July 2011)
C: the type of option (i.e., "call")
10: the option's strike price per share (i.e., $10); this can be one to nine characters (including decimals when needed)

Thanks to the menu-based trading platforms used by today's online brokers, you will rarely if ever need to type or recite to a broker a stock option contract's symbol when placing an order. But understanding the components of option symbols will empower you to cross-check the option holdings in your account and quickly recognize and correct trading errors when they occur.

Much in the same way that you determine the number of shares of stock you can afford to buy, before you proceed with your stock options purchase you will first need to determine the number of stock option contracts you can afford to buy. Option contracts for every available strike price and expiration date combination are quoted by bid and ask price (no different than stock) in the Options section of a company's Yahoo! Finance quote page. A single option contract represents control over one hundred shares of a company's stock, and the price of an option contract is quoted on a "per-share" basis. So the cost to purchase a call option contract representing one hundred shares that is quoted on Yahoo! Finance at $1 (per share) would be $100 ($1 per share × 100 shares).

> Option contracts, which represent one hundred shares of stock, are quoted on a "per-share" basis, so you must multiply the quoted option price by one hundred to determine the actual price to purchase or sell the contract.

Back to the Emerging Youth Apparel Company. It is New Year's Day 2011 and, while reviewing your holiday credit card statements, you find yourself amazed at how much your daughter has managed to spend at the "value-priced" apparel retailer. In just a few weeks, the retailer is scheduled to publicly report its sales and profits for the prior three-month period. If your intuition and due diligence are correct, the retailer's recent explosion in popularity among teen girls seeking value-priced, high-fashion apparel will fuel an unanticipated rise in sales to the surprise of Wall Street, which has long questioned the company's untraditional marketing tactics and retail store layout. The company's stock trades at $10 per share. Your options are: purchase shares of the company's stock or purchase call option contracts on the company's stock.

You already know how you would go about placing an order to purchase shares of the Emerging Youth Apparel Company's stock. Now let's review the steps you would take to purchase call option contracts for the company:

1. First enter the company name "Emerging Youth Apparel Company" into the Get Quotes field in Yahoo! Finance (finance.yahoo.com) or your online broker's Web site to retrieve the company's stock symbol, EYAC, in addition to the current market ask price of $10 per share.

2. Click on the Options tab to view a listing of all the company's available option contract strike prices and expiration months. Choose the highest available strike price that is equal to or less than the stock's current trading price (in this case, $10) and an expiration month approximately six to nine months out (in this case, July). Retrieve the symbol for the call option contract you are seeking to purchase (EYAC110715C10) in addition to the option contract's quoted per-share asking price ($1).

3. Multiply the quoted per-share asking price ($1) by one hundred to determine your actual cost per option contract ($100).

4. Not including broker commissions (usually $12–$50 for options), divide the total amount of money you want to in-

vest in the option contracts ($3,000) by the actual cost per option contract ($100) to determine the number of call option contracts you can afford to purchase ($3,000/$100 = 30 call option contracts, for control over three thousand shares of EYAC).

5. Since the market for buying and selling option contracts is not as large or as active as the market for buying publicly traded stocks, when purchasing or selling option contracts I generally recommend using limit orders (and usually under the guidance of a representative at your online broker). When placing the limit order, call or visit your broker's branch, or log on to their Web site and place "a *limit* order to purchase thirty September-expiration call option contracts on stock symbol EYAC at the $10 strike price at a contract limit price of $1 good for *today*." You are essentially saying, "I would like to make an offer of $1 per share to purchase the contractual right to purchase up to three thousand shares of stock in the Emerging Youth Apparel Company at a set price of $10 per share anytime between now and the third Friday of July. My offer is valid only until the close of market today." When the time comes to sell, simply place "a *limit* order to sell thirty September-expiration call option contracts on stock symbol EYAC at the $10 strike price at a contract limit price of (*insert current contract bid price*) good for *today*."

6. Confirm over the phone, by visiting in person, or by logging onto your brokerage account, that your order was executed and that you are the owner of thirty September-expiration, $10 strike price call option contracts on the Emerging Youth Apparel Company.

If, over the following six-month period, the Emerging Youth Apparel Company's stock price were to appreciate by 50 percent, to $15 per share, your $3,000 stock purchase would return a profit of $1,500 (300 shares × $5 profit) while your $3,000 call option contract purchase would return a profit of $12,000 (3,000 shares multiplied by $5 profit minus the initial $3,000 cost of the option contract). Not a small difference. If the stock were to double in value, your stock investment would return a profit of $3,000, compared to $27,000 for the options investment.

> The larger the stock price increase, the more you benefit financially from owning call stock option contracts versus shares of a company's stock.

Now suppose that over the entire six-month period, the company's stock either remained constant at $10 or dropped in price to $8. In this scenario neither investment, the stock or the option, would result in a profit. But unlike your option investment, which would expire worthless (resulting in a loss of $3,000), your stock investment would, at the $10 price, retain 100 percent of its original $3,000 value, or, at the $8 stock price, 80 percent of its original $3,000 value (a loss of $600).

> The larger the stock price decline, the more you are financially penalized owning call stock option contracts versus shares of a company's stock.

WHEN GAME-CHANGING INFORMATION
IS NEGATIVE

Investors often use a technique known as "short-selling" to benefit financially from stocks they anticipate will go down in value. The downside to short-selling a stock is that—unlike with purchasing stock or even purchasing call option contracts—one's potential losses are unlimited.

A "put option contract," on the other hand, will achieve the same effect while ensuring that the holder of the contract never loses more money than that which was originally invested.

Put Option Contracts

A put option contract is essentially the exact opposite of a call option contract. Whereas a call option provides the owner with the right (but not the obligation) to purchase a specific number of shares of a stock at a predetermined price and within a certain period of time, a put option contract provides the owner with the right (but not the obligation) to *sell* a specific number of shares of a stock at a predetermined price and within a certain period of time.

Put option contracts are often purchased as a form of short-term insurance by investors seeking to limit the potential losses on stocks they already own. You can also buy a put option contract on a stock you do not own. This is the investing equivalent of purchasing insurance on someone else's beach house because you believe it will soon be destroyed in a hurricane, or on someone else's car because you believe the owner is destined to get into a car accident.

> ### Put Option Contracts
> Unlike call option contracts, which rise in value along with the rise of a company's stock price, put option contracts rise in value when the price of a company's stock falls.

The strike price on a put option contract is the predetermined price at which the owner of the contract may sell shares of the given company's stock. A put option contract (the right to sell stock) with a strike price (guaranteed selling price) that is less than the company's current stock price will be priced based purely on the call option contract's remaining time value. A put option contract with a strike price that is greater than the company's current stock price will be priced according to the contract's intrinsic value plus any remaining time value on the contract. The higher the strike price, the more expensive the contract—which, if you think about it, makes perfect sense.

You can appreciate how the cost to own a put option contract giving you the right to sell someone gas at $5 per gallon would be more expensive than a put option contract giving you the right to sell someone gas at $1 per gallon. Who wouldn't prefer, and be willing to pay more for, the option to sell gas to someone at $5 rather than $1?

> A put option contract provides you with the legal right (but not the obligation) to sell stock at a predetermined price.
>
> A put option contract with a strike price that is *greater than* the company's current stock price ("in the money") already has intrinsic value, provides a small to reasonably large

amount of leverage, and will expire worthless only if the stock price rises above the contract's strike price.

A put option contract with a strike price that is *less than* the company's current stock price ("out of the money") has zero intrinsic value, can provide an extraordinarily large amount of leverage, and will expire worthless unless the stock price falls below that of the contract's strike price.

As with call option contracts, I nearly always buy my put option contracts that are "in the money"—that is, contracts in which my predetermined selling or strike price is greater than the company's current stock price. When purchasing put option contracts, I generally seek out the lowest available strike price that is equal to or greater than the current stock price of the company in which I am seeking to invest.

If all this is starting to read like déjà vu, it is because all the many rules we previously learned for purchasing and selling call option contracts also apply to put option contracts—just in reverse.

Suppose the previously cited chance encounter between your co-worker's nephew and the owner of the city's Major League Baseball team in a neglected part of the city was instead an encounter with a team of highway engineers from the State Department of Transportation that took place in a community park surrounded by one of the city's nicest neighborhoods. What if, instead of a billion-dollar baseball stadium development, the conversation being overheard involved a "not yet publicly announced" billion-dollar state highway project to supplant the neighborhood's posh community park? The houses currently bordering the park would lose their million-dollar greenway views in favor of a concrete wall bordering a 24/7 barrage of noise and air pollution.

You could use this game-changing information to purchase put option contracts on the houses bordering the park, providing you the right to sell those properties at a set price based on their value today. This set selling price would surely be higher than the price of the properties once word got out of the planned highway project. The ability to use a put option contract to contractually lock in a selling price for a defined period of time benefits you in a scenario in which you foresee an investment declining in value—just as the ability to use a call option contract to contractually lock in a purchase price for a defined period of time benefits you in a scenario in which you anticipate an investment increasing in value.

As an information arbitrage investor, you will find yourself with many more opportunities to invest with call options than with put options, but it is equally important to have knowledge of how put option contracts work, should the information arbitrage opportunity ever present itself that allows you to benefit from a company's demise. Remember, it was a put option contract on Snapple stock that enabled me to monetize my first information arbitrage observation at the age of seventeen.

BIG REWARDS COME WITH BIG RISKS

It is important to note that with every stock option investment, regardless of the contract's strike price and expiration month, there comes a real possibility of losing all—and by "all" I mean 100 percent of the money you originally invested—and much more so than if you were simply to purchase shares of stock in a company. Hence the importance of making this type of leveraged investment from a Big Money account funded with Other People's Money: money you are not afraid to lose, risk-averse money that is specifically earmarked for greatness. Even so, it is rare that I will put at risk more than 50 percent of the funds in my Big Money account in any single option investment.

Every investor needs to determine the level of risk that is most appropriate for him. My options strategy in relation to picking a strike price, expiration date, and proportion of available funds to risk is designed to serve a single purpose: to maximize my investment return for information arbitrage opportunities that I am supremely confident will result in the directional move of a stock. Stock options may sound like a complex financial instrument reserved for the financially savvy, but when fully understood and properly used, they are nothing more than simple tools of leverage that can become a small investor's best friend.

10

LIFE WITH INVESTOR'S GLASSES

When my wife, Amy, was pregnant with our twins, she e-mailed me an article from her expectant moms' club about an innovative new baby bottle that eliminates a newborn's intake of air bubbles. Her note to me read, "Investment opportunity?"

As the star of my trend-spotting network, I can always count on Amy to wear her investor's glasses. Meanwhile, the two of us made a sizable investment in our quest for a restful night's sleep by purchasing our first "all foam" mattress from Tempur-Pedic. For years our orthopedist had been trying to persuade us to make the switch from a spring to a Tempur-Pedic foam-supported mattress. We had resisted purchasing a Tempur-Pedic mattress due to the extreme denseness (and associated firmness) of their patented TEMPUR® pressure-relieving memory foam material, a longtime love-it-or-hate-it attribute touted by the company.

What recently sold us on the idea was the company's newly formulated Cloud line of mattresses, which features a pillow-soft top layer of lighter-density memory foam. Apparently, our preference for both comfort and support in a foam mattress was widely shared by others. The hour we bought our mattress, we were one of three couples visiting the mattress store to purchase a Tempur-Pedic Cloud-series mattress among dozens of competing mattress options. According to the store manager, the Cloud line had become the store's number-one requested mattress—nearly doubling the store's sales of Tempur-Pedic mattresses since the launch of the line a year earlier.

The new mattress line was a particular hit among women, who, according to the store manager, in general favor a softer-feeling mattress. I soon discovered that the store's sales of Tempur-Pedic mattresses weren't the only thing that had doubled that year. In the twelve months since launching the crowd-pleasing Cloud line, Tempur-Pedic's stock price had climbed from $15 to beyond $30 per share—which made me wonder . . .

How many people in my vast personal and business networks had, while mattress shopping over the past year, come into contact with or perhaps even purchased a Tempur-Pedic Cloud mattress? One, three, ten? How many times had I walked past a mattress store in the past year? How many opportunities had I had to uncover the game-changing information that had been sitting in front of me begging to be discovered?

One of the few experiences shared among all self-directed investors is the array of defining first moments—both positive and negative—that each of us experiences as the result of making our-investment decisions. That moment could be the frustration of a missed opportunity or the fate of that first winning stock pick we made and researched entirely on our own. It could be the first time one of our investments doubled in value or, of course, the first time we were forced to take a significant loss on an investment mistake.

Only by experiencing these peaks and valleys for yourself will you acquire the strength and resiliency to become a true self-directed investor. That is, an investor who is capable of both interpreting and acting on information he uncovers with dogged confidence, even when such information mandates going against the sweeping tide of Wall Street.

Now that you, too, have a shiny new pair of investor's glasses, nothing will ever look the same. Like that first time you viewed high-definition television, even the most mundane moments of your daily life will become interesting. But as with any new pair of glasses, your eyes will need some time to adjust. So if you find yourself stumbling across more than one or two great information arbitrage investment opportunities this next year, slow down—you might be setting yourself up to be the victim of your own wishful thinking.

I've shared with you my many mistakes so that you will not repeat them. But that's what you shouldn't do. Here's what you should do:

- Exploit Wall Street's vulnerability. Focus your efforts on products, companies, and trends (female, youth, low-income, rural) viewed as foreign to Wall Street's core demographic of middle-aged, affluent men who work and reside in major metropolitan areas.
- Believe what *you* see, not what financial pundits and those on Wall Street tell you to believe.
- Research your investment observations with the vigor and rigidity of a scientist seeking to submit a breakthrough

discovery to a prestigious scientific journal—pursuing only *game-changing* investment observations that are *not yet widely known or accepted as fact by Wall Street.*

- Institute the 100× money multiplier across every area of your life to unveil new sources of Other People's Money for funding your Big Money account.

- Let the concept of Big Money investing with Other People's Money empower you to act on the investment opportunities you uncover, and use stock option contracts to maximize the potential return for each of your investment dollars.

- Sell your investments the second the game-changing information becomes common knowledge—whether that be at a profit or a loss.

- Start small, but start now. Keep in mind that I started with just $300!

- Above all, remember that you are not alone. Exponentially increase your observational and due diligence resources by leveraging each and every person in your daily life, and those you are able to connect with through social media, business networking, and online investment communities.

The key to prospering as an information arbitrage investor lies in one's ability to quickly uncover and process game-changing information. Goldman Sachs and Morgan Stanley have their research departments, but we self-directed investors have one another, and together we outnumber and out-diversify all the world's investment "experts" and "professionals" combined. Internet-based communities provide us with the collective scale and means to corroborate game-changing information more quickly than any Wall Street firm.

Immerse yourself in life. Connect and regularly engage with family, friends, colleagues, and children. Read weekly tabloids. Never miss an opportunity to watch a blockbuster movie. Keep up with the evolving landscape of products, media, entertainment, and culture as it intersects with you and those in your life. (The following chapter shares the stories of people just like you who learned to monetize the world around them as self-directed investors.)

View your world with the perceptiveness of a private investigator, the inquisitiveness of a scientist, and the patience of a big-wave surfer. You can't chase the Next Big Thing, but by being astutely observant, you can be sure to recognize the Next Big Thing before those on Wall Street do. And when you do, you will know exactly *what* to do, *how* to do it, and *when*!

11

SUCCESS STORIES[†]

Stories of real, self-directed, amateur investors who outsmarted Wall Street abound! Here's just a sampling.

THE POWERS OF OBSERVATION

Chris Stone owned a small business that built trade show displays. In 1996, when the marketing manager of a company he'd never heard of called wanting to buy an exhibit to use at a couple of small trade shows, Chris was happy to meet with him. The situation seemed like nothing out of the ordinary: just another small company looking to do some trade show marketing.

---

† With their permission, I have revised the following stories submitted to InvestorVillage.com by individual investors.

Over the next twelve months, however, Chris saw the small company, Getty Images, continue to add to their trade show exhibit arsenal and increase the number of shows they attended. He decided to read up on Getty and learned that they licensed stock photography, which was something he was using with increasing frequency as large-format printers made it easier to produce big images for trade show booths. Chris also saw that Getty was aggressively adding images to its online catalog, making it easier for people to buy and use stock photography.

In 1999 he decided to invest, making a sizable purchase of Getty stock. Getty was on a historic growth path, consolidating a fragmented industry through strategic acquisitions. They capitalized on the tsunami of stock photography usage led by the explosion of companies that were building Web sites. Chris eventually sold his stake in Getty, realizing a significant seven-figure return.

PHYSIOLOGY OF SURGERY

During medical school forty-five years ago, Laurent Lucas often went to the hospital library to read whatever books he could find. One of those books, by a British author, had the title *Physiology of Surgery*. As he read, he learned that many of the problems of surgery have nothing to do with the operation itself but with narcosis, blood loss, and creating access to the operative field. For example, a coronary bypass in itself is a very minor and harmless operation. What is not harmless, and may be life-threatening, is the necessity of opening the thorax by cutting muscles and sawing bones, which results in blood loss, prolonged pain, impaired respiration, and a surge in stress hormones. Dr. Lucas remembered fellow students telling him that it was useless to read such a book, "because you don't need to know that information for examinations." In fact, he never did any surgery.

In the 1990s, computerized surgery arrived in the marketplace. Remembering what he had learned from his student days, Dr. Lucas immediately realized that such machines could reduce many surgical problems. He invested most of his available money in the companies Computer Motion (ticker symbol RBOT) and Intuitive Surgical (ticker symbol ISRG), and then waited patiently and stubbornly for their success—against the advice of many skeptical observers.

Eventually the success came. The two companies merged, the value of their shares doubled, and Dr. Lucas sold half of them to lock in some profits. The other half made him a return of about $3 million. Laurent has no regrets reading *Physiology of Surgery*, even if he was never able to use this knowledge for any medical school examination.

DISNEY MAGIC

Charles Edward's family made several trips to Disney World in the late 1970s, and like so many others, Edward became devoted to the Disney experience as the best way to spend his vacation dollars. He marveled at how this company seemed to really get it right, and saw an organization that appealed to diverse people, made them happy, and caused them to want to spend excessive amounts of money without any reservation.

He chose Disney as an experiment. He felt it had potential simply because its product made people happy. He bought Disney stock and held on to it for nearly twenty years, turning a profit of roughly thirty times what he had paid for the stock. He will forever have a deep admiration for the Disney Company and Walt personally, for giving him many "magical days."

INVEST IN WHAT YOU KNOW

In 1971, right out of college, Ken Goodgold was fortunate to secure an engineering job with AT&T. The thrill soon wore off, however, as they quickly put him to work in "Operator Services." This decades-old department was dominated by women who would sit for hours with printed phone directories looking up the telephone numbers for a never-ending stream of customers. The inquiries never stopped; information switchboards are a 24-hours-a-day, 7-days-a-week, 365-days-a-year operation.

To the casual observer, call volumes may appear random. A disciplined engineer, however, can accurately forecast call volumes by season, day of the week, or even time of day. Most calls are placed in the "busy hour" (BH). The time it takes an operator to respond to a typical call is called the "average work time" (AWT). Ken, along with other AT&T engineers, designed complex programs to predict how many operators would be required for each hour of the day, and which hours each individual operator would be assigned. This was no small task, for in those days, large cities such as Dallas required thousands of operators.

Ken found the work tedious and unfulfilling. He did, however, enjoy working with numbers, and never ceased to be amazed by the significance a small difference in the "average work time" would make to the number of operators required. For instance, if the AWT of the team of operators in Dallas could be lowered by one second, the company would save $2.5 million annually. He knew this because he had made the calculations himself.

So imagine his excitement when two start-up companies designed systems that would replace the paper operator records with computers and automated databases. While the products varied in approach, design, and cost, each promised to shave at least 10 seconds off of the AWT of the operating teams. And at 2.5 million seconds per city per day, how could AT&T afford not to buy the equipment? Ken bought a lot of stock in both start-ups.

As it turned out, AT&T spent a small fortune with both companies. The value of Ken's investment tripled. But more important, he learned a valuable lesson: keep your eyes open and put some money on the table when you think you have it figured out.

DNDN PIRATES

In early 2009, while living in an ecosystem where the first U.S. biotech industry was born, the San Francisco Bay, Thanh Hoang sensed in his blood that a new golden age of biotech was about to dawn. As a first-generation MBA student at UC Berkeley with no medical or biotech knowledge, he started following biotech investors with successful track records across multiple message boards. He was very fortunate to stumble across a strange but very knowledgeable New York bio-investor who identified himself as a pirate. This "pirate" sought out hidden treasure by researching and investing in little-known biotech companies. As the two bonded through many silly postings and information-sharing experiences, Thanh began calling him the "captain" of a like-minded group of biotech investors who would name themselves the DNDN Pirates. Thanh Hoang became their stock board manager.

Why DNDN Pirates? They all met at the Dendreon (ticker symbol DNDN) message board of the InvestorVillage online investing community. Through statistical projections and the collaboration of pirates and the community, they were able to outsmart Wall Street.

The pirates had taken a heavy position in the biotech company Dendreon, which, in May 2010, would become the first company to receive FDA approval for a cancer immunotherapy treatment. Not a single Wall Street analyst who followed Dendreon's clinical trial predicted the company would receive FDA approval. Since the FDA had not once in its history granted approval for a cancer immunotherapy treatment, Wall Street had all but dismissed the company's immunotherapy treatment as pseudo- or "junk" science. While terrified investors were scrambling to sell their DNDN stock shares in the low $2 range, at the strong recommendation of nearly every Wall Street analyst covering Dendreon's stock, the pirates were accumulating the stock based on their own due diligence.

Then came April 2009. The company snagged major media headlines with positive drug trial results! The stock immediately shot up to the $20 range—and would eventually go on to trade as high as $55. The DNDN Pirates owed their newfound wealth to their online community. From the hard work of a stay-at-home dad, an ex-nurse, two cancer survivors, an enthusiastic day trader, several engineers, a "ruthless girl," and an MBA student to the firepower of a retired grandpa, these "pirates" depend on one another to identify and properly evaluate biotech investing opportunities. Their duties include, but are not limited to, attending presentations, researching medical journals, scouring medical blogs, and interviewing patients and medical professionals.

Today they share pirate jokes and give one another advice on personal issues. They have magnified their early riches by riding many more triple-digit-return investments in the biotech industry. The DNDN Pirates are about more than just making money. They have become friends. Once lost in a world of finance, they have found extraordinary investing success—and that success did not come with their mimicking those on Wall Street, but instead by leveraging the one infinitely valuable asset that Wall Street lacks: a varied and un-biased insight into the real world.

Appendix

AN INVITATION TO WALL STREET'S UNDERWORLD

The following message board excerpt, titled "Would Whole Foods buy OATS?" was posted by the pseudonym Rahodeb on the Yahoo! online stock bulletin board for Whole Foods. OATS is the stock symbol for Wild Oats Market, the largest natural foods grocery competitor to Whole Foods. The message, speaking to the likelihood of Whole Foods acquiring Wild Oats Market, reads:

> Almost surely not at current prices. What would they gain? OATS locations are too small . . . OATS has lost their way and no longer has a sense of mission or even a well-thought-out theory of the business. They lack a viable business model that they can replicate. They are floundering around hoping to find a viable strategy that may stop their erosion. Management clearly doesn't know what it is doing. . . . OATS has no value and no future.

Rahodeb's post went on to speculate that Wild Oats would likely slide into bankruptcy and had no chance of being acquired by Whole Foods until its stock fell below $5.

Contrary to Rahodeb's viewpoint, just two years later Whole Foods would go on to buy Wild Oats Market at a price of $18.50 per share. Ordinarily, a message board user "getting it wrong" would be far from a newsworthy event. But what if the user who posted the message were in fact the purchasing company's CEO?

John Mackey is the CEO for Whole Foods. His wife's name is Deborah, a name whose letters, when jumbled, spell "Rahodeb." Over a seven-year period from 1999 through 2006, John Mackey made more than 1,300 anonymous postings on the Whole Foods and Wild Oats Market message boards under the alias Rahodeb. Was his intention to spread information to the detriment of his competitor in the hopes of acquiring OATS at a lower price? According to Mackey, "I posted on Yahoo under a pseudonym because I had fun doing it . . . The views articulated by rahodeb sometimes represent what I actually believed and sometimes they didn't. Sometimes I simply played 'devil's advocate' for the sheer fun of arguing. Anyone who knows me realizes that I frequently do this in person, too."

This now-infamous message board posting sparked a firestorm among conspiracy theory types, who, along with millions of self-directed investors, battle one another for dominance and credibility across thousands of investor message boards.

As amateur investors, we are light years removed from the daily machinations of Wall Street information gathering. Our days are spent engrossed in our own careers or home lives, not mingling around the water cooler with institutional financial analysts and staff traders. But between serving customers, seeing patients, preparing school lunches, or making sales calls—or perhaps during our lunch breaks, and especially late at night, when our kids are fast asleep—we can log onto our favorite stock's message board and engage in both information sharing and spirited debate with other self-directed investors.

Much in the way that blog reporting has become a threat to traditional news outlets, stock bulletin boards have evolved to challenge traditional financial media and advice channels, forming a living, breathing community of self-directed investors with diverse skill sets and areas of expertise. It is not at all uncommon for boards to include vendors, clients, and even former and current employees of the companies under discussion. These people and groups are frequently more "in the know" than even the most connected Wall Street analysts and traders.

But as evidenced by the "Would Whole Foods buy OATS?" posting, the unregulated nature of stock message boards can create an inhospitable environment for any new self-directed investor attempting to navigate Wall Street's underworld. How do you know if you are reading the viewpoints of another amateur or a company insider? How do you know if such viewpoints are ingenuous or made with deceptive intent?

GETTING YOUR VIRTUAL FEET WET

"Opportunity is missed by most because it is dressed in overalls and looks like work."

—THOMAS ALVA EDISON

Knowing how to naturally engage and communicate with the varied cast of characters who make up stock message board communities is more learned than innate. The established protocol, jargon, and hidden agendas of message board veterans make for a less-than-hospitable environment for ill-prepared message board newbies. But with proper training, anyone can learn to successfully navigate and monetize this great underworld of Wall Street, where the potential for information discovery is nearly endless.

It is my experience that most anxiety (at least in its milder forms) related to public speaking can often be linked to a lack of familiarity with one or more of the following: subject matter, environment/context, and rules of engagement. This lack of familiarity (most often the result of a failure to prepare oneself) tends to undermine the speaker's confidence and leads her to fear being judged or found wanting by her audience.

In some respects, message boards are the online equivalent of public speaking. Many investors taking a peek at stock message boards for the first time are often intimidated by the thought of having to interact publicly on these forums, especially with investors who seem to know the ropes. There are a number of common causes for this discomfort, including:

- Being a slow typist, you are afraid you won't be able to keep up with the pace of the conversation.
- Being a lousy typist, you are afraid your posts will be filled with typos/misspellings.
- Being unfamiliar with the tools, you don't know how to post messages.
- Being unfamiliar with the industry, you're unsure of the accepted lingo.

For example, a friend may have turned you on to a particular biotech investment, but you never liked science in school and therefore don't have a firm grasp of the fundamentals of the science behind the company's cancer-fighting drug—even though you may have a nursing background and you like the company's prospects based on the need for the company's product that you witness daily among your patients. As you can see, you may have something meaningful from your own background to contribute to the online conversation (remember our discussion of "coopetition"), but if you shy away from the message boards because you are embarrassed about your shortcomings in one area, then everyone potentially loses out on getting a more well-rounded appreciation of the given investment opportunity. By keeping your virtual mouth shut, you might be inadvertently depriving others of important information you can bring to the table regarding the consumer market (or lack of one) for the treatment in question. And by not asking questions, you may be left in the dark and vulnerable to misinformation.

Maybe you are afraid of making an idiot of yourself in front of thousands of message board users who might judge your every word. Maybe you are afraid of being "flamed"—that is, being sent offensive, insulting messages. Perhaps you have a tendency to become too attached to your online "persona," and you personalize any disagreements or discussions.

Remember that online you are anonymous; your audience can't "see" you and they certainly can't "hear" you. They don't know or even want to know your real name. You are just one of many with the common goal of collectively gathering and sharing intelligence.

The good news is that adequate preparation can overcome any such perceived deficiencies or anxieties and allow you to step out onto the field of battle armed with the same weapons (knowledge) as other participants.

The rest of this chapter is designed to address those feelings of inadequacy or lack of preparedness. My goal is to educate you as much as possible about the mechanics of reading and posting messages to online message boards. I want to give you the knowledge and tools that will allow you to derive the most value possible from an online environment teeming with game-changing information.

MESSAGE BOARD JARGON FOR NEWBIES

The quickest way to get up to speed is to get a handle on the lingo or jargon used by investors on the typical stock message board. As with a lot of newer communication technologies, the shorthand used often seems like a foreign language to anyone who didn't grow up speaking it. Getting exposed to the language and having the tools to translate it will help alleviate any anxiety you have about participating in an online conversation with other investors.

The number of acronyms you are likely to encounter on stock message boards varies greatly from one board to another, but one thing is clear: the more time you spend on these boards, the more acronyms you are likely to run into. As a general rule, these acronyms can be placed into three levels (with overlap, in many instances):

1. **Acronyms related to online messaging itself.** For example, you might see ROTFLMAO (Rolling on the Floor, Laughing My Ass Off) posted on boards, and in text messages on cell phones. Other common acronyms related to online messaging include EOM (End of Message) and IMHO (In My Humble Opinion).

2. **Acronyms related to the niche universe of stock investing.** You will frequently see abbreviations such as CC (Con-

ference Call), ASM (Annual Shareholders Meeting), DD (Due Diligence), FUD (Fear, Uncertainty, and Doubt), SP (Share Price), PPS (Price Per Share), MB (Message Board), BOD (Board of Directors), and BK (Bankruptcy).

3. **Industry-specific acronyms.** For biotechnology, you might see ASCO (American Society of Clinical Oncology) coming up with some frequency, whereas in the energy sector, you might see messages referring to the IEA (International Energy Agency).

Add up all the potential acronyms out there and you are easily talking tens, if not hundreds, of thousands. The good news is that there are many handy free acronym translation tools on the Internet, such as acronymfinder.com, that will do all the translation work for you.

CAST OF CHARACTERS

As is the case in just about any genre, from tales of old with their knights in armor and their damsels in distress to TV Westerns with their gun-slinging cowboys on horseback, stock message boards have their own cast of familiar and rather predictable characters. The following list is by no means exhaustive, but it does represent several of the more common character types you are likely to see on any active stock message board:

The Newbie

As the name implies, a newbie is someone who is new to something. That seems simple enough. For our purposes, there are three likely ways the term is relevant. First, it may describe someone new to stock investing. Second, it may refer to someone new to the peculiar world of stock message boards. This person may be entirely comfortable and well versed in managing his or her money in the market, but simply unfamiliar with the nuances of public digital communications. The third type of newbie is someone new to a given stock. So whether you are new to investing or to stock messages boards, you can still find yourself a "newbie" in relation to other investors who have been following a particular stock for a longer period of time.

Of course, a newbie can be any combination of the three, including being new to all three. The good news is you don't stay a newbie for long. All it takes is a little gumption to get yourself out there, and a little practice to get the hang of it, and before long, you'll be the one spotting other newbies—and lending them a helping hand.

Viewed from the perspective of the established community (or audience of posters and lurkers), the newbie has a legitimate reason to feel anxious. Many newbies are afraid of being embarrassed, afraid of the reaction of the established community or network. In a lot of ways, it's just like being the new kid in school. People are social animals. We tend to be skeptical of new things and uncomfortable with change. We are likely to question the new guy's motives—especially when they seem to be at odds with our own. We are likely to challenge the newcomer.

Don't fall prey to this sort of mentality. Don't shortchange yourself by avoiding the newbie in online conversation. Sure, it's easier to keep quiet and not ask questions that you are afraid others will think are silly. But then, you are the one who will lose out. After all, the only truly dumb question is the one you never ask. By not asking, you leave your answer to chance—you'll either never get an answer or you'll have to wait until someone else asks the question.

No matter what your background, chances are you will have

something unique to contribute to the conversation, whether you're a nurse who understands how a particular type of cancer is currently treated in a real hospital environment or a mortgage title clerk with a unique insight into the fluctuating market for new home loan applications. My message to you is: Be unstoppable! Don't let fear or uncertainty get in the way of your success.

The Troll

This particular "character" comes in many varieties, but all trolls have one thing in common: they are a pain in the neck for anyone interested in following legitimate dialogue on the forums. You may have heard of high-frequency computer trading thanks to the infamous 2010 "Flash Crash," when the stock market fell over a thousand points in minutes. If high-frequency trading didn't cause the crash, it almost certainly contributed significantly to it. Well, the message-board troll is essentially a "high-frequency poster."

The Board Hog

One type of message board troll is the board hog. As his name implies, the board hog tends to monopolize the online conversation. Board hogs need to be the center of attention. Without proper supervision or enforcement by the management of the message board in question, a board hog may end up literally "killing" a board by driving serious posters away. For example, a board hog might post a particular stock's change in share price every five minutes throughout the day, so a series of his posts might look like this: "XYZ up another 5 cents," "Uh-oh. Spoke too soon. Down 8 cents now." Followed by another one ten minutes later: "Up 2 cents. We're green, baby!" The board hog does this either to be the center of attention or to render the board useless to serious investors.

A different example of a board hog is someone who uses the board the way one uses Twitter, giving updates about where he's getting his haircut or what he's having for lunch—stuff that no one else really cares about. Again, the idea is that he's just cluttering up the board.

Sometimes board hogs come in groups, so that one group essentially exhibits the same behavior, usurping the board and using it for their own discussions, while driving all "outsiders" away.

Board hogs post messages nonstop—sometimes for attention, sometimes to disrupt the flow of information when the conversation of the board supports a point of view that is in opposition to their own. Many board hogs post completely off-topic messages, treating the board more as their own blog rather than as a shared space. The more disruptive messages tend to be about religion and politics. The good news is that once you've identified a board hog, you have the ability to hide his posts, using the message board's Ignore User feature.

The Fudster

The term *Fudster,* also written as *FUDster,* is derived from the acronym FUD, for "Fear, Uncertainty, and Doubt," the Fudster's stock-in-trade. Newbies are especially susceptible to Fudsters, who are disinformation specialists. Common tactics of the Fudster include: (1) bringing up negative issues that may have been resolved years ago and are no longer relevant; (2) quoting unreliable sources; and (3) fabricating false information "by accident or mistake."

Fudsters will often engage in argumentative attacks known as flame wars: questioning, challenging, and casting doubt on the integrity of many of the most respected posters on a given board. On top of that, they will rarely respond to challenges to their own integrity, motives, or research. As with many other species of troll, the Fudster will have his or her own agenda or reason for plying his craft, which more often than not is simply to support his own investment position, be it positive or negative, on the particular stock being discussed.

Let's say the CEO of a company you are researching is named John Smith. Everyone knows John Smith went to Harvard and is a stand-up guy and an excellent businessman. But the Fudster will intentionally post a link to information on a "John Smith" he obtained through a Google search suggesting that Smith is, say, a convicted felon. The Fudster's message will read something like this: "You'd have to be crazy to buy stock in a company run by a guy like this . . ." The reason this sometimes works is that many retail investors lead busy lives and don't have time to dig deeper, so when they read something like "convicted felon" in the same sentence as a name they know from company management, they just move on.

Be suspicious of any message board poster who is less than 100 percent transparent in his research or who is reluctant to provide proper supporting documentation to back up his claims.

The Spammer

Trolls who post links and information designed to promote everything from penny stock newsletters to Rogaine and Viagra are categorized as generic commercial spammers. Often a posted link will look like it is going to take you to a legitimate article about your stock, only to redirect you to a page promoting the spammer's wares.

Other spammers are of the stock-promotion variety. They may be a group hired to "spread the word" about a particular stock. This is often, though not always, done in conjunction with efforts to "pump and dump" the stock, a form of illegal market manipulation. Other times the spammer is a lone individual who simply has his own agenda, such as garnering more attention for a stock he already owns. The purpose could be to determine if other investors will agree with the poster, in the belief that more investor "eyeballs" will lead to more demand, particularly in the case of thinly traded stocks of smaller, lesser known companies.

Spammers often use catchy e-mail subject lines to hook their prey, such as "Hey, nice action on this stock today," followed by a post that goes something like "You should really check out this penny stock newsletter. It's the best one around. I've been a subscriber for years. Worth every penny, no pun intended."

Make use of the Ignore User and Report Abuse message board features to reduce the amount of noise caused by spammers.

The Short

Being short means that you have made a directional bet on a stock and that direction is "down" or "lower" than the price the stock traded at when you "sold short." There is nothing inherently bad about the Short, as his opposing point of view generally provides a needed sense of balance to stock message boards.

The Long

Being "long" on a stock is what most people associate with investing. That is, you like a company for any number of reasons and you buy its stock believing it will go up over time. But this also comes with a clear bias. The Long is positive. Some would argue that this leaves him susceptible to wearing blinders and being led (or perhaps misled) by the company or even by other blind followers (Longs).

Message board posters are often accused of being short or long based on their sentiment—either expressly conveyed, for example, by identifying their long or short bias, or by so stating in the body of their messages. However, you should exercise a lot of caution when considering making such a conclusion. Many longs have legitimate questions and are nervous or concerned, and looking for answers. That in and of itself doesn't make them "short." Often the Long for a particular stock board has spent years tracking and researching the underlying stock and is more than happy to share his knowledge with you and point you to historic posts or conversation threads to help bring you up to speed on a stock's history.

The Basher

This is a poster who is not only overtly negative on a stock, but aggressively, relentlessly, and often insidiously negative. The Basher is not above misleading other investors for his own gain. He tends to be very confrontational and abusive, spewing curse words and engaging in personal attacks against other posters, rather than engaging in more civilized debate.

Here is an example of a typical "bash" or basher post (i.e., essentially a baseless opinion with an in-your-face negative spin, with nothing offered to back it up and effectively no redeeming value): "This company is a complete POS. The BOD are a bunch of crooks. Got a friend who works there. Says it's going down in flames. Word on the street? BK. Yup. TIMBERRRRR."

The Pumper

Also known as "cheerleaders," pumpers contribute seemingly benign or innocuous posts singing the praises of management or company developments without the slightest shred of critical thinking applied. In other words, no real due diligence accompanies their giddy (and possibly blind-faith) support for a company. More pejorative synonyms for the Pumper include Pied Piper and Pump-'n'-Dumper, someone who "pumps" (hypes a company with misinformation to inflate its stock price) in order to then dump shares on unsuspecting investors before they become aware of the company's true worth.

An example of a post from a typical Pumper (i.e., a baseless opinion with an over-the-top positive spin, with nothing offered to back it up): "I LUV this Company!!! Been in the market 28 years. Best management team I've ever bet my hard-earned cash on. Major contract any day (sorry, can't reveal my source). Going to the MOON, baby!"

Don't be surprised when you see "bashing" and "pumping" online. Posts like this one shouldn't necessarily discourage your interest. After all, each investor has his own agenda. If you are "long" on the stock, you want it to go up. You'll benefit/profit when you are able to sell it at a price higher than the one you paid when you purchased it. So promoting/touting the benefits of the investment tends to attract buyers you can sell to. On the other hand, Bashers may be actively short-selling the stock, in which case they benefit when the share price falls. They also may be looking to "bash and buy"—that is, they actually like the stock, but don't want to pay the current price, so they feed you negative information so you'll unload your stock at fire-sale prices. A Pied Piper/Pump-'n'-Dumper could also be trying to help artificially bid up the price of a stock they don't like so they can short it from a higher price.

To avoid being taken advantage of, it is critical that you never take anything you read on a message board at face value. It can be difficult, even for board veterans, to determine with certainty whether a particular member's posts are sincere or driven by a hidden agenda. Seek out the concrete information in posts that is provable, and be wary of emotional, nonspecific rants—and of posts made by company board members, who do not have a documented history of quality message board contributions. Treat the information you discover on message boards the same way an investigative reporter would deal with a potentially newsworthy hot tip. Be suspicious of "confidential sources," do your own homework, and discard any and all information you are not able to verify by independent sources.

What might initially appear to be bashing could be someone's way to get negative information out. The environment is combative. But information from a Basher can force you to dig deeper and think harder. Bashers will challenge your assumptions and make you double-check your work.

The Experienced Trader

This person could be a former broker or trader, or just someone who's been around the block. The Experienced Trader can help you understand the mechanics of investing. For example, he could probably tell you how and when the cash dividends of a particular stock will be paid to its investors.

The Resident Board Expert

This is a self-proclaimed expert, such as a doctor or lawyer with specialized skills in the relevant field of a particular company. Resident Board Experts are often the most valued message board members—for their ability not just to uncover game-changing information early as insiders in their respective industry but also to interpret potentially game-changing information that they or others on the board have uncovered. If you are looking for a second opinion on an idea or discovery you've made, seek out Resident Board Experts. They are generally eager to assist others to the best of their ability.

Veteran Longs (aka Long-term Longs)

These are people who have been following a particular stock for a long time, usually measured in years. Anyone who has been on a message board for a while will be able to identify these users. Long-term Longs may believe in a company's underlying benefit to society and are willing to wait patiently, often for many years, to see their expectations delivered (and their dreams come true). These people are also more likely to get to know one another and truly gel as an online surrogate family of sorts—versus the flippers and traders who are there only to study and exploit the short-term price movements of a stock and couldn't care less about the underlying company/business.

The Lurker

The Lurker isn't exactly a character but, rather, a presence. This person is more like the audience member at a play, or the silent observer at the community school board meeting. The Lurker sits at his computer monitoring the activity on the board, reading messages, but not engaging the community of active posters. Lurkers are akin to the "silent majority." If human nature is any guide, there's a very good chance that the number of investors "lurking" around a given stock message board is many times the number of posters actually contributing information via messages.

MIXING AND CONFUSING THESE TERMS

Many people mistakenly mix together different elements of the terms *basher* and *short, pumper* and *long*. They are quick to think that anyone who bashes a stock must also be short the stock. However, the Basher can be independent, in much the same way that a "Blue Dog" Democrat can be fiscally conservative and a "Log Cabin" Republican can be socially liberal. In other words, a so-called Basher may in fact be long. The motivation for his bashing could be to manipulate the price of the stock downward temporarily in order to purchase additional shares at a low price. And a Short may legitimately "short the stock" because he honestly believes the company is on the ropes or the stock price is unsustainable (or whatever the negative issues may be). Therefore, negative questions or comments may not qualify as "bashing" at all, even though many Longs (that is, investors effectively on the other side of the trade, so to speak) may accuse the Short of bashing their stock. The better you are at spotting the nuances of each message board character type, the easier it will be for you to filter and interpret each user's posts. For example, the post "our local Best Buy had a line out the door longer than I had ever before seen" is more credible and therefore potentially more significant coming from a known message board Long than from a known message board Pumper, as the Pumper is prone to exaggerate.

NETIQUETTE

Let's imagine we are invited to a dinner party. For the moment, let's not worry about who's throwing it, where it's being held, or even what the occasion might be. If you and I attend this imaginary party, we already know ahead of time that certain social conventions will apply and certain expectations must be met. This is part of our normal "socialization." Rules of common decency (some written, and many unwritten but equally understood and no less important) must be obeyed. The Golden Rule of "do unto others as you would have them do unto you" is not a bad one for any social situation.

In the case of a dinner party, if I get drunk and start calling you names, I risk embarrassing and offending the other guests and angering the host. I also risk being asked to leave or perhaps even be escorted out against my will. If I become belligerent, it would not be out of the question for the host to call the police.

Obviously, rules will be more relaxed at a Super Bowl party among a bunch of college buddies than at a wedding reception for a local dignitary. But even at the Super Bowl party, there will be limits to what is considered acceptable behavior and what has clearly gone over the line, wherever that line may be drawn.

A common understanding of acceptable behavior should be no different in an online forum—although, sadly, it often is. For some reason many people, including otherwise professional people who manage money for a living, seem emboldened by the anonymity of message boards and forget their manners when engaging other investors.

Common examples of poor "netiquette" include:

- posting in ALL CAPS
- posting a long subject line
- not properly labeling an "off-topic" post (such as a comment on current events or politics)
- cursing
- engaging in flaming or personal attacks
- "outing" people (i.e., posting their real names)
- failing to put EOM ("end of message") at the end of a short subject line that does not lead to a post with additional content (thus causing the reader to waste time clicking to a blank post)

The downside to indecent, uncivil, or otherwise abusive behavior on stock messages boards may include any or all of the following:

- The poster's message risks being deleted by the Website owner. (Many boards have a way for readers to report abusive behavior, and each forum has its own level and manner of enforcement.)
- The poster's account may be terminated by the service provider and the poster blocked from future registration.
- The poster may simply turn people off to the point that they will "ignore" him, meaning they will no longer read what he writes. This may not seem as harsh as the first two possibilities, but it means that the poster is no longer part of the online conversation, and may miss out on the opportunity to get his hands on game-changing information.
- Similarly, the poster may find that she is now a pariah on the board. No one wants to talk to her. Once she has offended the community, it will be difficult for her to get other investors to answer her questions.
- In extreme cases, the target of the poster's abuse may seek legal action against her. Although there are difficulties involved in doing so—subpoenaing records, hiring an attorney, attempting to prove actual damage—the injured parties are often investors, and, as such, they tend to have more financial resources than the average Internet user.

Legitimate questions, civilly asked, should be addressed in a fair manner on any message board service. If a poster is ugly and rude to other posters just because she thinks she can scare someone out of his position, she will be hard-pressed to make friends on a message board (or any other online venue, for that matter). The opposite is equally true: if a poster tries to misinform people by lying to them with sweet-talking baloney, assume that her reputation will catch up with her.

BOARD MANAGEMENT 101

So, now you've met the cast of characters, you're up on the jargon, and you understand the basic guidelines for proper board etiquette. What's next?

Highly active stock boards tend to have dozens, if not hundreds, of posters contributing content to them each and every day—in real-time. A heavily visited board on Yahoo! for popular stocks such as Apple and Google might have thousands of messages posted to it in a single day. In part, this is because (as discussed in the previous chapter) Yahoo! Finance tends to have few curbs (if any) in place to slow down a user's ability to set up multiple accounts and dominate (or, at the very least, disrupt) a board's discussion. Of course, it is also due to the fact that Yahoo! Finance is still the place most investors turn to first for their information. By contrast, smaller communities such as Motley Fool, Raging Bull, and InvestorVillage, with their tighter curbs and lower volume of traffic, might have hundreds of messages posted in a single day on a heavily visited board. (As I suggested earlier, there is a good chance that the quality of information, relative to the quantity of messages posted, is higher on smaller community message boards than on Yahoo! Finance. But that's simply my opinion.)

The bottom line is that busy boards pose an information management problem for busy investors. If you are like many millions of other self-directed investors, you have a day job. You have lots of responsibilities. At home. At the office. With your professional organizations or volunteer activities. You might literally have only a few minutes during your lunch break to hop online to see what the latest buzz is. So it can be very frustrating when you find a board littered with trash talk.

Fortunately, tools on sites such as InvestorVillage and Yahoo! Finance can help you manage the volume and frequency of messages, to reduce unwanted information and improve your ability to keep up with desirable information. Common tools to help a self-directed investor get the most out of any stock message board service include the following:

Ignore Lists

An Ignore List allows you to hide messages from posters that you feel have no value and are simply a waste of time. Some sites limit the number of poster names that you are allowed to maintain on your ignore list. One remedy, should you happen to reach your limit, is periodically to review your list and remove names of the less offensive to make room for the more egregious abusers.

Off-Topic Message Filtering

The ability to filter messages marked as "off-topic" can also very useful. The big issue here is poster compliance. If posters fail to properly identify a message as "off-topic" you won't necessarily be able to easily avoid it.

Favorite Member and Favorite Message Tracking

Some sites allow you to tag posters and messages as your favorites, and will even provide an automated RSS data feed of syndicated Web content that you can then customize to include your favorite board and/or posters. This allows you to receive a streaming feed without even having to visit the Web site. Some feeds will e-mail posts to you as they occur in real time. That way you won't have to be logged into your account or even at your computer. If you have a smartphone, you can check your e-mails while you're out of the office and on the go.

Be careful not to overuse these tools, as they might cause you to miss important posts. For example, when you put someone on "ignore," you will no longer see his messages. The danger in doing this is that sometimes the most annoying poster can end up making the most insightful observation. If you have him on ignore, you may not realize that he has contributed meaningful information until other posters on the board comment on it (assuming they do).

Still, sometimes it simply comes down to making a calculated trade-off. If you're really pressed for time, it doesn't make sense (or it may literally be impossible) to sift through all the noise hoping for one nugget of game-changing information buried in the longest message or a string of messages by an obnoxious poster.

The good news is that the wisdom of crowds tends to help the good information rise to the surface. And even if someone who reads faster and/or has more time to spend reading messages gets to it before you do, you probably still have an advantage over lots of other investors, because at least you're keeping up with the talk on the boards on a regular basis and not waiting for it to be picked up and repackaged by Wall Street analysts and mainstream journalists. This increases your chances of maintaining an information/time advantage, and enhances your ability to act on an information imbalance before information parity is reached.

LET COMMON SENSE BE YOUR GUIDE

As with almost any other important human endeavor, the use of stock message boards is fraught with risks and dangers. Your best defense is common sense. You use it when strangers ask you for money in a grocery store parking lot. And presumably you use it to spot spam, such as those e-mails from Nigerian princes with moneymaking schemes.

If you keep your guard up and view anonymous claims with a skeptical eye, you won't fall victim to these scams. And if you are equally vigilant and apply the same common sense and skepticism to claims on message boards, you won't fall for sweet-talking Pied Pipers or "the sky is falling" Chicken Littles, who offer no factual basis for their claims/positions/arguments. There is a lot of good information flowing on these boards. But there's also misinformation and scam artists trying to cheat you out of your money. They may try to talk you into buying a dud, or they may sell you a diamond in the rough just before it is cut, polished, and starts to sparkle.

Usually you can get a good sense of the integrity of posters by reading a handful of their messages. Most will betray their biases quickly. They tend to write about certain themes, and their tone and language are relatively consistent from one message to the next. If you have good intuition about other people, use that to your advantage. Go with your gut. It's usually quite accurate. Don't rely solely on the opinion of other posters—and be cautious about relying on artificial means of judging credibility. By this I'm referring to the reputation-scoring mechanisms some sites offer. Depending upon how well thought out these are, they run the risk of being easily gamed, and thus the very credibility they are intended to convey is vulnerable to attack and may be compromised.

If possible, ask the other person either publicly or privately how

215

long he has been following a particular stock. How did the poster find out about the stock in the first place? Does the poster think the share price is headed up or down, and why? Then sit back and see what the response is—assuming there is one. This will give you an excellent opportunity to evaluate the quality of the information being provided.

Asking such questions is an efficient means of accomplishing what investors call "due diligence," or DD. As I have pointed out elsewhere in this book, you can do your due diligence on the company itself. Likewise, you can do your due diligence on other posters, which is a must if you plan to collaborate with other investors online.

When speaking of claims made by his Soviet counterparts, President Ronald Reagan would often quip, "Trust, but verify." In the world of online stock message boards, I would modify that advice. Forget trust. *Verify* is the operative word here.

Your goal should be to reel in as much verifiable, objective, factual information as you can. Verification of the information is what matters. And it's what online tools, such as search engines, allow us to do much more quickly than ever before.

Information in and of itself is neutral. It may be good, or it may be bad. That's for you to figure out. If someone writes, "Silly Bandz are sold out at every toy store in my home town of Dallas," that's information you'll want to verify. Don't take some anonymous poster's word for it.

If someone writes, "This technology isn't that great. Five other companies have something better." Well, that's a little harder to verify. But you should try. For starters, you might consider challenging the poster (nicely!) to name the five other companies—or at least their products. If unwilling or unable to do so, that poster may be sharing erroneous information.

But don't stop with that conclusion. You still owe it to yourself to independently verify the situation. A simple Google search of each competing company should give you a good head start. Take a look at what each company has to say about its products. Next, see if you can find real consumer feedback and user reviews. Then go back to the message board and recruit the help of other investors. If a dozen of them come back with similar results in support of a particular point of view, that might be helpful, and perhaps even the deciding factor. At least now you have done the best you can and are not simply taking any one poster's comments as conclusive.

My wife and I spent our honeymoon at the Four Seasons in Maui, a beautiful resort well worth the small fortune it cost us to stay there. Thanks to candid traveler advice from ordinary vacationers I gathered on Tripadvisor.com, I knew better than to book one of the hotel's "mountain view" rooms, which actually have more a "parking lot" than a "mountain" view—a mistake I would surely have made had I relied on information provided by the hotel and travel guides alone.

What works for uncovering game-changing information and doing your due diligence on hotels also works for researching cars, restaurants, lawn mower oil, and, most important, investments. The Internet, along with the emergence of online networks and communities, has transformed our ability to gather, assess, and validate game-changing information as it materializes around us in real time.

A well-run Wall Street firm leverages the specialties of each of its associates. Unfortunately for these firms, many of its associates think and act much the same. When properly leveraged, the breadth and diversity—in terms of age, geography, and real-world specialty—of the people in your life and those you engage with on social networks and through message boards will reach far beyond that of any Wall Street firm.

Acknowledgments

I want to thank my mother and father for encouraging me early in life to chase big dreams. And to my wife, Amy, whose unwavering support through the years has helped me realize several of those dreams, including this book.

To my brother, Don, a stock options mastermind—thank you for teaching me the tools of financial leverage. Your lessons allowed me to monetize many of my first investment observations as a teenager with limited investment capital.

Nichole Argyres, you are my ideal editor and publishing partner for this book. I hope my book's lessons produce a fraction of the positive impact on your investing portfolio as your edits and guidance have had on my writing.

I will forever be grateful to Blue Kidd for his insight into investing social networks and the investing community he supports at InvestorVillage.com.

ACKNOWLEDGMENTS

I want to express my gratitude to the entire St. Martin's Press team and everyone who has made a contribution to the manuscript and book launch, especially Laura Chasen, Jeanne-Marie Hudson, Joe Rinaldi, Mark Fortier, Steve Gottry, Adam Sanders, David Hahn, Jared Sharpe, Ethan Friedman, and Stephen Hanselman.

Lastly, this book could not have been written if it weren't for my dear family, friends, colleagues, and supporters who have provided endless encouragement over the years. Thank you for believing in me and my unconventional investing philosophy. As we go about chasing our respective goals in life, I hope this book and its readers—by connecting, sharing, and critiquing investment observations on ChrisCamillo.com—will serve to greatly increase our collective chances at investing success.

Notes

1. Jack Grubman, *Grubman's State of the Union: Does He Ever Stop Talking?*, Salomon Smith Barney analyst research report, March 2001.
2. These lines were taken from a user comment to the *Fortune* article link www.tech.fortune.cnn.com/2008/10/22/apple-q4-earnings-analyzing-the-analysts/. The posting, which is still listed under the article at the time of this book's publication, was made by Brian from Irvine, Calif., Oct. 22, 2008, 12:04 PM.
3. William Goldman, *Adventures in the Screen Trade*, New York: Warner Books, 1983, p. 39.
4. Bill Barker, "The Performance of Mutual Funds," The Motley Fool, available at www.fool.com.
5. Standard & Poor's Indices Versus Active Funds Scorecard, www2.standardandpoors.com.

6. H. C. Engelbrecht and F. C. Hanighen, eds., *Merchants of Death: A Study of the International Armament Industry*, New York: Dodd, Mead & Company, 1934, pp. 69–70.

7. Srikant Dash, *Majority of Active Fund Managers Underperform Benchmarks—Across All Categories Over Past Five Years*, Standard & Poor's press release, April 20, 2009.

8. Vincent P. Carosso, *The Morgans: Private International Bankers, 1854–1913*, Cambridge, Mass.: Harvard University Press, 1987, pp. 94–95.

9. "Chapter 2: Birth of a Profession," *The Age of Independent Advice: The Remarkable History of the Independent Registered Investment Adviser Industry*, San Francisco: Charles Schwab Corporation, 2007.

10. David Grayson Allen, *The History of Scudder, Stevens and Clark*, New York: Scudder, Stevens and Clark, 1994, p. 7.

11. Pauline V. Young and Calvin Fisher Schmid, *Scientific Social Surveys and Research: An Introduction to the Background, Content, Methods, Principles, and Analysis of Social Studies*, New York: Prentice Hall, 1956, p. 107.

12. James Surowiecki, *The Wisdom of Crowds*, New York: Anchor, August 16, 2005, p. xviii.

13. James Surowiecki, *The Wisdom of Crowds*, New York: Anchor, August 16, 2005, p. xiii.